THE RUSSIAN TEA ROOM COOKBOOK

THE RUSSIAN TEA ROOM COOKBOOK

FAITH STEWART-GORDON AND NIKA HAZELTON

ILLUSTRATIONS BY RICHARD GIGLIO

INTRODUCTION BY CLIVE BARNES

A GD/PERIGEE BOOK

Perigee Books
are published by
The Putnam Publishing Group
200 Madison Avenue
New York, New York 10016

Library of Congress Cataloging in Publication Data

Stewart-Gordon, Faith.
The Russian Tea Room cookbook.

Reprint. Originally published: New York : R. Marek, © 1981.
Includes index.
1. Russian Tea Room. 2. Cookery, Russian.
I. Hazelton, Nika Standen. II. Title.
TX723.3.S79   1984   641.5947   83-25126
ISBN 0-399-51032-X

Designed by Helen Barrow
First Perigee Printing, 1984
Printed in the United States of America
5 6 7 8 9

To Jim

Contents

THE
RUSSIAN TEA ROOM
COOKBOOK

Introduction

BY CLIVE BARNES

THE ONLY PEOPLE who cannot remember their first visit to The Russian Tea Room are those unfortunate souls who have not yet been to this unique pleasure palace on New York's West Fifty-Seventh Street, a few steps from Carnegie Hall. For, once through those handsome revolving doors, delight awaits, and your first encounter with it should be as memorable as your first kiss.

Twenty-five years ago I was initiated into the Tea Room by the great Russian dance editor Anatole Chujoy. Charming and irascible, a major personality in the world of dance, he had arrived in the United States in the mid-twenties, just prior, in fact, to the arrival of The Russian Tea Room itself. In Russia, particularly before the Revolution, tea rooms were an institution, with a social function rather like the English pub or the Viennese coffee house: they were meeting places for gossip, rumors, rumors of gossip and gossip of rumors, with the special ambience of kindred spirits in a spiritual home where—quite incidentally—pastry and tea were served to the gossipers. From the first, The Russian Tea Room was intended as a kind of hangout for the emigré White Russians, refugees from the Soviet Revolution—not just a home away from home, but a home away from the home they had lost.

From the beginning, in a little shop across the street from its present splendor-filled location, The Russian Tea Room attracted a clientele associated with the arts—and looking back, it's not difficult to see why. In the wake of the Revolution, musicians, dancers and actors who had once performed in St. Petersburg and Moscow began to come to New York—among them, for instance, Chaliapin, the opera star, and the great dancers Mordkin, Lifar and Fokine, who introduced New Yorkers to the vanished splendors of the Imperial Russian Ballet. For these artists and their admirers, The Russian Tea Room was the place to assemble, talk about the theater, exchange stories, relive past glories and spin out future fantasies. Non-Russian artists, finding this exotic atmosphere charming and electric, followed in their train.

In its early days, The Tea Room had a number of different owners. In 1932, Sasha Maieff, former owner of a halvah factory in Moscow, bought it. And it was he who extended its epicurean charms beyond the earlier realms of tea, chocolate, pastries and ice cream. He began serving full meals—and, indeed, initiated the great New York tradition of Russian food at The Russian Tea Room.

Equally important was Maieff's decision, when Prohibition was repealed, to rip out the old soda fountain and replace it with a bar, whose specialty, of course, soon became vodka, in all its authentic and mysterious diversity. The Russian Tea Room was growing up.

In 1946, The Tea Room was acquired by a group of partners, including the late Sidney Kaye (né Kalmanovitch), who, in 1955, secured sole control. From this inauguration of his imaginative leadership dates the beginning of The Russian Tea Room as we know it.

From the beginning, Anatole Chujoy, my mentor, was a regular, and so was that great impresario Sol Hurok. They helped to establish the restaurant as the common meeting ground for dancers and musicians. Chujoy never tired of comparing the place to Cubat's in St. Petersburg—a restaurant where dancers and their admirers would repair after performances at the Maryinsky to talk about the evening's performance and the price of diamonds. Chujoy ate at The Tea Room twice a day, six days a week and once on Sundays and, on the most conservative of estimates, he is reputed to have consumed 25,000 meals there before his death in 1968. He had his own booth—the first one on the left as you entered—from which he could scrutinize everyone who came in and, more importantly, observe with whom they left at the night's end.

On my own first visit—that first kiss—I was immediately fascinated. I had never seen such a curious place in my life. (Of course, regulars, myself now among them, take its quixotic eccentricities in their stride.)

I noticed the long bar (replaced since by a handsome new shorter one) and opposite, several tiny booths, in size certainly more suitable for a lovers' tryst than a business lunch. Between the booths and the bar was likely to gather an enormous line of thronging would-be patrons hoping for a stray table (incidentally, this is a place where, however famous you may think you are, you always book ahead—or stand in line) and goggling in the meantime at the various interesting lunching parties. Over the door I noticed a wonderful clock, one of the three famous Tea Room clocks. As I have since discovered, they may all suggest a slightly different time. If you idly wonder which is right, you will come to realize—as I have after many visits—that in their own way they are all right but, like the artistic clientele itself, just a little temperamental, unlike the service, which is always impeccable, unobtrusive and warmhearted.

I recall that on my first visit I took the opportunity to excuse myself to go to the men's room merely because of my fierce curiosity to see the rest of the place. I assumed, correctly, that the rest rooms would be at the back (since changed to fancy new ones upstairs), so I started my procession and threaded my way through the blood-red leather of the banquettes and chairs, the daisy-pink napery, the magnificent confusion of pictures, flowers and samovars, those legendary and timeless Christmas decorations (kept on all year)—all balls, baubles, and glitter—and, of course, the people. It doesn't do to stare, of course, especially when you're a visitor from London, as I was at that first blush. However, I did notice that the clientele, dressed in an Aladdin's Cave of varying styles and fashions, all looked extraordinarily interesting. Although I kept my eyes politely to myself, I did catch a glimpse of Maria Tallchief, then the reigning goddess of the New York City Ballet, who saw me and smiled. I returned to Chujoy with a flush of triumph. "I just bumped into Maria," I said as casually as I could. "Yes," he replied, "she came in twenty-two minutes ago." Gosh, did he keep a log book! That was the moment I made my vow to return as often as possible, a promise to myself I have never regretted.

In 1967, after a long illness, Sidney Kaye died. Faith, his widow, a South Carolina girl whose acting career had taken her to Hollywood and Broadway after graduation from Northwestern University, now took charge. She found herself from the outset faced with the realization that she had a mortgage, some insurance money, and the news that her husband had had to sell a chunk of the business. Should she continue The Tea Room or let it go? Like Scarlett O'Hara after the destruction of Tara, she decided to deal with the problems one day at a time: The outside interest with the chunk of the business was paid off with the insurance money—almost all of it. Improved business took care of the mortgage, and very soon her own special touch—which held more than a hint of magic—was turning The Russian Tea Room into one of the most successful individually owned restaurants in Manhattan. Indeed, like so much else, The Tea Room since my first forays, has changed a great deal—but, surprisingly, unlike much else, almost always for the better. It is remarkable that, in spite of the changes and its new prosperity, The Tea Room's vital heartbeat has remained the same. It is still a haven for artists and lovers of the arts. The food is better than ever. The ambience remains, yet there is an elegant new image: the polished wood, the luminous brass, the mirrors shine brighter than ever. The paintings are new and more interesting. A whole new room, the Cafe, has opened upstairs, beautifully maintaining the atmosphere and look of the original restaurant downstairs (in fact, sometimes I prefer the Cafe's roominess). It can be used for private functions as well as overflow. The whole design of the restaurant has been revitalized—but its feeling is unaltered.

Food and service are the vital core. The first is, of course, in great part Russian, the second a delightful and special mixture of informality and care. At a time when too many New York restaurants are either snooty or slipshod, The Russian Tea Room shines like one of the bright lights in a naughty world.

Its horde of smiling waiters in red Russian tunics and busboys in green are all expertly supervised by the manager, the totally unflappable and smilingly imperturbable Gregory Camillucci, assisted by the equally admirable dining-room manager, Rosa Forand. These two ensure that the welcome is genuinely welcoming, that the service is smooth, that the many famous people, from rock stars to best-selling authors, who eat here are part of a family of guests, never bothered by autograph seekers, but never insulated from the rest of the guests either. All enjoy The Tea Room's comfortable luxury. Lunchtimes The Tea Room becomes an informal club for deal-making producers and directors, while hopeful starlets with dazzling smiles spear their low-calorie salads and wait to be tapped on the shoulder by fame. Although there are no statistical records to confirm this, the educated presumption is that any lunch at The Russian Tea Room that takes place in one of the bar or dining-room booths and includes a star, a producer, an agent and a director is inevitably a prelude to a Broadway show or movie.

Dinner is a more sober affair as theater and concert goers pour in for the first seating at 6 P.M. At 7:45 they are replaced by the political heavyweights, foreign notables, and just plain hearty eaters of The Russian Tea Room's specialties drawn from the pre-Revolutionary Russian cuisine and prepared in one of The Tea Room's two kitchens. By 9:45, when the second wave of diners has worked its way through Irish salmon, Borscht, Zakuska, Shashlik, and any other of the 117 dishes on The Tea Room's menu—topped off with pastry so rich that it tastes as though it had been prepared for a regiment of sweet-toothed grand dukes—there is a momentary lull. Then, at 9:55, the brightly polished revolving doors begin to spin again as phalanxes of returnees from early concerts, lovers in search of close quarters for tender touchings, and gaggles of Madrileños from Spain who never sit down to eat before 10 P.M. begin to arrive. By 11:00 or even later, the line waiting for tables still stretches snakelike to the door. At 12:30 the last diners and topers are being served, and from 1 A.M. (2 A.M. on Saturday) until 11:30 the next morning The Tea Room is closed, while a squad of cleaners and brass-polishers gets ready for the next day's onslaught.

To carry the burden of serving between 1,000 and 1,400 meals a day it takes a staff of 150, which is drawn from twenty-two countries and speaks a total of forty-four languages. To keep The Russian Tea Room in workable shape because of the press of business (carpets that might, in other restaurants, have a life span of perhaps three years, last about eight months in The Tea Room), there is an additional outside force of eighty-three cabinetmakers, stonemasons, carpenters, plumbers, steamfitters, refrigeration engineers, and a number of other skilled workers. And the samovars have to be polished by the four-man force of brass polishers. So do the copper and brass bowls. And the masses of flowers have to be arranged daily in those bowls. A restaurant is food, drink, people . . . and a lot of work to be done and redone each day.

Of the food and drink you are going to read enough in the following pages. What I will say here is that after eating in The Russian Tea Room it was a grievous disappointment to eat in Moscow and Leningrad. Eventually, I admit, I discovered through that wonderful Russian hospitality that eating in private homes there was another thing altogether. But apart from a few specialty restaurants—a wonderful Georgian place, for example, in Moscow—there are no restaurants I encountered in Russia to match The Russian Tea Room.

What to eat in this cornucopia of Slavic delights? Well, locked as I am in my eternal and unequal struggle with the weighing machine, I permit myself to have Blini with Red Caviar and Sour Cream once a year. Chicken Kiev is superb. I love, too, that marinated saddle of lamb called Karsky Shashlik Supreme (although, sign of the economy, portions have gotten a bit smaller of late), the hot and cold borscht—both with hot piroshki (lovely little pastries), the Eggplant Orientale and so much more. Try some of the other Russian specialties, such as the simple, almost humble, Cotelette Pojarsky (the beef and veal patties), or, if you like, those lamb patties called Luli Kebab. Try some of the special specials, such as Wednesday's delight, the Siberian dish Pelmeny (really a soup with meat dumplings and dill) served with sour cream and mustard sauce. Then there is that aristocrat of fish dishes, the fish *en croûte* called Kulebiaka.

The menu varies during the year, everything not being on every menu, but there is one time it positively explodes—during the great holiday, Russian Easter, traditionally a very special time in the Russian calender . . . and at The Tea Room. Those extraordinary bits and pieces called *zakuska*—which you will learn to make from the recipes inside—are served then. These were originally intended to break the fast in Russian Orthodox homes after the midnight Mass that ushers in Easter Sunday, holiest of the Russian holy days. Of course, a simplified form of zakuska is always on the menu, but at Easter, simplification goes out the door, and the zakuska arrives in its richest, most succulent and diversified version.

If you have a sweet tooth, The Tea Room—shades, perhaps, of its soda-fountain youth—is always ready. During the Easter holiday, those classic Russian confections, *Paska* and *Kulich*, are available every day. Apart from being basically indescribable, the paska is a noble yellow mound with the consistency of a coarse mousse. It is made of cream,

puréed pot cheese, almonds and little bits of candied fruit, chiefly cherries and angelica. Kulich, shaped like a chimney pot, is a yeast cake mixed with nuts and raisins. Traditionally it is blessed in Church on Easter before being eaten.

Sweets are always special. The Tea Room has its own bakery—one of the few restaurant bakeries left—and the assorted pastries are excellent, as is the traditional fruit compote (not to be confused with anything of a similar name elsewhere!). Russian cream, a sort of Russian blanc-mange, is wonderful too, as is *kissel*, a sweetened cranberry purée served with light cream. None of these is for the dieter, however, who would do better to pass straight on to the wonderful coffee and tea (the latter perhaps in a glass with cherry preserves or vodka).

Of course, for Russian food, you need Russian chefs, right? Well, if it were right, this cookbook could serve a truly useful purpose only if printed in Russian. No, the Russian cuisine is far too good a thing for the Russians to keep to themselves. Nowadays only two or three members of the staff are Russian, and only one, Svetlana, is concerned with the preparation of the food. In fact, the last Russian chef hung up his *toque blanche* in 1977. Since then the "Russian" chefs have been French, Japanese, Hungarian, Puerto Rican, and American.

What to drink with all this Russian food? There is a good and reasonably priced wine list, and the French carafe wine is highly drinkable. However, Seymour Britchky, my friend and fellow Tea Room devotee, and New York's most perceptive restaurant critic, says bluntly in his three-star review: "Vodka and champagne are the drinks to drink. Vodka is ordered from the Vodka menu." It is indeed. And the vodka is properly served here: in a specially designed miniature decanter, neat and ice-cold, nestling in its own bed of crushed ice. With caviar, it's unbeatable; without caviar, it's very good—and cheaper. And caviar brings one to champagne, which is this ambrosial food's other natural partner.

Champagne is one of the few wines that is consistently better the more it costs. The Russian Tea Room offers some of the finest French champagnes, and I particularly recommend the Dom Perignon and the Perrier Jouët.

Of course, restaurants are not merely a matter of food and drink. For the people who work in them, and the people who eat in them, they are also a matter of memories. And the very mention of Dom Perignon brings back one very old but oddly pungent memory to me. *Esquire* magazine was doing a pictorial feature on what certain theater folk liked to do about eating after the performance. We were a pretty varied bunch and made some pretty varied choices—some, such as Beni Montressor and Zubin Mehta, electing to dine at home. I selected The Russan Tea Room—and a photo session was set up. I was to be

pictured eating *nalistniki,* which are basically crepes filled with pâté and mushrooms.

Obviously the photograph had to be taken after the night's guests had more or less left and the kitchen on its last legs before closing. That suited me well enough. I went to the theater, went on to my office to write the next day's review, killed time with a couple of drinks in a neighborhood bar, and arrived at The Tea Room at the appointed hour. I had not had a meal since lunch. The photographer was setting up his lights and his little white umbrella, and after greeting Faith, I sat down in a booth. My food arrived immediately—and so did the food editor from *Esquire.* She rushed in and, without batting an eyelid, started to spray my food with what I took to be hair spray. I must have looked aghast. She cheerfully said something like "Oh, that's makeup." That much even I could see, but what was it doing on *my* food?

It seems, and what an innocent I was, that food when photographed doesn't really look like food unless it is slathered in invisible, inedible goo. Those nalistniki were not for eating. They were for photographing. Faith, the perfect host, instantly produced a bottle of Dom Perignon. Her charity gave me the hope that all was not lost. Disliking to drink alone, I offered to share it with the photographer. And then, as the photographs seemed to be taking a rather long time, we shared another bottle.

All this time the photographer was arranging and rearranging his lights—often with the camera in one hand and champagne in the other. I told him this was the best photo session I had ever had in my life. He responded by telling me that he had never met such an apt subject. The night was young, and by now the flashbulbs were flashing. Oddly enough—a clear case of God looking after babies and drunks—the photos came out fine, and one was duly published in *Esquire*. Yet another, suitably framed, found its way onto The Tea Room's elegant green walls, where, at time of writing, it still clings over the second banquette on the left. Look at it closely. The nalistniki are a fake, the Dom Perignon in its cooler is genuine, and the glazed look around my eyes is by courtesy of Messieurs Moët et Chandon and the ever resourceful Mrs. Faith Stewart-Gordon.

I have so many memories stored up about The Tea Room, as do all those who eat there—most of them memories of fun and good fellowship. I have eaten there with theater people, with legions of ink-stained journalists and even with regular writers. But, of course, for me it is the dancers and the dance world that stand out. Nureyev, Bruhn, Alexander Grant; Nadia Nerina, Makarova and many other of the Soviet Russians. But of all, the one who truly stands out in my memory is Sol Hurok: "S. Hurok Presents." Hurok was a strange and very lovable man. I knew him well when he was right at the end of his career. Although he had the habit of telling the same stories twice—sometimes during the same meal—his mind was really laser-sharp. Everything I know about the ballet business, as opposed to the ballet art, I learned from him. I had lunch with him two days before he died and he was very busy planning ahead, as ever. About a week earlier my wife and I had a late supper with him in The Tea Room. As always, he started with smoked salmon, and he talked. He always talked, about the past from Pavlova to Fonteyn, from de Basil to the Bolshoi. Dogmatic but fascinating.

The unfancy, nonpatronizing attitude of the staff I have mentioned before, but as I end, I cannot resist mentioning it again because it is so much a part of The Tea Room's far from mysterious mystique. Take this for example. Once in a while, perhaps only once in a lifetime, you hear in reality something funny that eventually becomes debased into a popular joke. It was at The Tea Room that I actually heard with my own, admittedly flapping, ears, a well-known but somewhat naïve film director order "One Perrier and soda—on the rocks." Gregory Camillucci, the Manager himself, was taking the cocktail order—and he did not twitch a muscle or bat an eyelid. That is democracy in action. The Russian Tea Room treats everyone alike—even the rich and the foolish.

FAITH STEWART-GORDON BY AL HIRSCHFELD

The Russian Tea Room—A Celebration
BY FAITH STEWART-GORDON

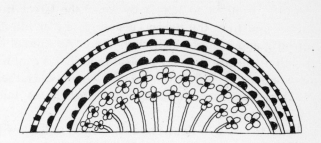

OVER THE YEARS so very many people have asked for a cookbook from
our kitchen that it is a great pleasure indeed to present at last *The
Russian Tea Room Cookbook.* The Russian Tea Room represents more than
half a century of continuity and history in a very special place; a special
restaurant, it has come to mean even more than that to many people—a
place to meet, to drink, to visit and to celebrate.

We have been especially fortunate to have Nika Hazelton, one of the
most highly respected and widely read cookbook writers in America,
take on the Herculean task of translating The Russian Tea Room's
recipes to home cooking. But The Russian Tea Room has proven that,
in fact, Russian food does not have to be prepared by Russian chefs. It
can be learned as easily as any other cuisine, and our own international
kitchen staff has adapted itself very well to the largely hearty and
straightforward dishes that lurk behind such exotic names as Kasha à la
Gurieff and Pelmeny Siberian.

Russian food has, in fact, many similarities to American food—if you
translate the Russian use of sour cream (largely used because it did not

spoil like butter in pre-refrigeration days) to our preference for cooking with butter. The classic Russian cuisine created in pre-Revolutionary days, before 1917, is composed of Scandinavian, Mediterranean-Baltic, Georgian, Armenian and Eastern Mongol elements. It borrowed strongly, too, from the French, German and Dutch cuisines of the eighteenth century, brought to Russia by Peter the Great from his European travels, and from the Italian cuisine via the architects who built St. Petersburg and brought their chefs there. All this, of course, intermarried with the hearty Russian peasant food that is centuries old in origin—the wonderful borschts, for instance, about which there's an old saying: "There are as many recipes for borscht as there are grandmothers in Russia!"

Indeed, a glance at a map of Russia and its borders will show readily how many imported elements there are in Russian cuisine. Still there are always certain specialties that come to mind when we think of Russian food—vodka, caviar, tea served from a samovar, blini, shashlik, and for those who know, the divine sweet twins, Paska and Kulich.

Combining versions of many of these dishes is the great classic hors d'oeuvre platter, zakuska (meaning, literally, "small bites"), which originated as a full table of food in the country houses of nineteenth-century Russia, when travel was difficult and people arrived after a long journey to find waiting, day or night, a huge spread of hot and cold dishes to revive and sustain them. Zakuska are really accordion-like in versatility; they can consist of two or three fish items and pickled mushrooms, or they can be two full tables heavily laden, one a cold table with five kinds of caviar, fish of every description, Eggplant Orientale, stuffed eggs, and cheeses, and a hot table with pâtés, mushrooms in sour cream and tiny piroshki, baby meatballs and pirogi. In addition one must consider the variety of vodkas consumed along the way. But in the nineteenth century the zakuska table was itself only the prelude to a seven- or eight-course meal served with wines or sometimes French champagne. In Russia, mealtimes have, in any case, always been a movable feast; dinner could be served any time from 2 to 8 P.M. When dinner was early, say at six or before, a supper at ten would follow, and this was no mean snack in itself. I believe this is why The Russian Tea Room has always divided meals carefully into lunch (11:30 A.M. to 4:00 P.M.), dinner (5:00 P.M. to 9:30 P.M.) and supper (9:30 P.M. to 12:30 P.M.); and the "supper" really means to most diners a late dinner or after-theater supper.

Caviar (from the Turkish *khavyah)* is the egg, or roe, of the Caspian Sea sturgeon. Both Russians and Iranians fish these waters, and due to pollution, war and illegal fishing, the supply of beluga, the largest and most beautiful caviar egg, has become rarer and more expensive. Add to this the fluctuations of international currencies and you can understand why these large, lightly salted eggs (beluga malossol) are more of a delicacy than ever. Slightly less expensive and smaller in size is the Osetra, whose taste can be just as good as the Beluga. Then there is Sevruga, a still smaller size and still of good quality; and pressed caviar, imperfect eggs, quite salty, like a paste. Many people like the pressed very much as a spread with Blini or on toast. Red caviar, salmon roe, also varies in quality. But the eggs should always be bright orange-red and firm. It is much less expensive than black caviar and delicious with blini because of its salty flavor—and because you can afford to eat more of it! We buy red caviar by the barrel, black caviar in 14 ounce tins so that it will not remain open too long before it is used up. Caviar must never be frozen, but it must be stored below 42° F. Unopened it can keep for weeks—once opened, only a few days. (Turn the can upside down when closed, to mix the oils, and never buy pasteurized caviar— it has been processed and is no longer fresh.)

The samovar, in which tea was traditionally made and served, was brought to Russia by the Tartars—nomad Mongols who traveled across Asia, brewing their tea as they went. Samovar actually means "self-cooker." Hot water, not tea, is brewed in the samovar over charcoal, and then tea leaves, which are kept in a small teapot with a little water, are added to the boiling water to make tea. In Russia, tea was drunk in a glass by men, it is said, and in a cup by women. But not very many homes had cups and saucers anyway!

The Russian Tea Room has a splendid samovar collection,

about ninety samovars in all. They are displayed in red-and-gold niches in the dining room and in the Cafe upstairs and add a shimmering quality to the decor, resembling miniature Oriental castles in all shapes and sizes. Someone once said to me, "You ought to display some balalaikas" (the Russian musical instrument that looks like a lute). But I said, "*These* are our balalaikas—the samovars. You won't find anything more Russian than these!"

Indeed the decor, the whole look, of The Tea Room is part of its great charm and its attraction to so many people, not only from New York but from all over the world. My husband, James Stewart-Gordon, and I have gathered together a sizable collection of original paintings, which have also become one of the restaurant's outstanding attractions. We love looking for new pictures and new ideas for The Russian Tea Room, and we have traveled to many countries to search them out. Years ago we felt that the original Art Deco decor of The RTR dining room could be restored and enhanced by gilding the wooden curtains that frame sections of the room and by adding mahogany, marble and brass to set off the red banquettes, the pink tablecloths and the green walls of the dining room. So, the paintings we choose are mostly post-Impressionist, Russian, Art Deco and American School of the 1920s and 30s, with a few mavericks like Beryl Cook, a contemporary English "naif," to liven things up. Like everyone else's, our tastes change, and some of the pictures come and go, but gradually we have assembled a strong nucleus that expresses the mood of The Russian Tea Room, its history, and the vibrancy of the patrons who have loved it along the way.

The Russian Tea Room changes, yet it retains its spirit and its charm. It has, of course, come a long way from the original little room where only tea and pastries were served to White Russian emigrés of the 1920s. But we bring to each new generation of patrons a feeling of continuity and joy in renewal. I remember the first time I came here in 1955 and met my late husband, Sidney Kaye, who was then the owner. His contributions to the traditions of The Russian Tea Room were my natural inheritance—the challenge was left to be fulfilled. I am deeply grateful to my husband, James Stewart-Gordon, who helped me have the courage to keep the faith—and who had the vision and understanding to help me shape and realize so many of my dreams for The Russian Tea Room.

Many people have played a part in making *The Russian Tea Room Cookbook* a reality. But I especially want to thank Pat Loud, my literary agent, who truly got this long-time project off the ground; Joyce Engelson, our editor, who envisioned the book so long ago, as did publisher Richard Marek, and James Beard, who gave his wisdom and generosity in the early stages of our project—a real friend; Gregory Camillucci, our manager, who has contributed much time and trouble; to our chefs and all The Russian Tea Room staff, past and present, and especially to Cyndi Dunleavy, my secretary—many many thanks.

About the Recipes in This Book
by Nika Hazelton

WHEN I WAS ASKED to adapt The Russian Tea Room recipes for home cooking I undertook the job because The Russian Tea Room was familiar territory. For many years, I have enjoyed Russian food, not only here but in Moscow and Leningrad, Paris and Berlin. But before I explain how I went about my task, let me quote Faith Stewart-Gordon: "This is not a diet cookbook or a quick-preparation cookbook. Here we want to make traditional and classical Russian recipes from The Russian Tea Room kitchens available to the home cook."

For this reason the book concentrates on The Russian Tea Room's Russian recipes. Like all great restaurants, The Russian Tea Room serves not only its specialties, but also the whole gamut of traditional American foods such as omelets and other egg dishes, grilled meats, salads, sandwiches and fresh fruits. These dishes are beautifully prepared, but their recipes are familiar to all good cooks. I therefore have omitted most of them from this book, and concentrated on the recipes that are not familiar to all good cooks, that is, the special recipes of The Russian Tea Room.

Throughout the book, I have adhered faithfully to the original concept of The Russian Tea Room recipes. I have stood in the hustle and bustle of the busy Russian Tea Room kitchen, watching the chefs and taking notes on their work. As you may realize, restaurant cooking, which is prepared for a large number of people, differs considerably from cooking for a family or a small party of guests. The job is not simply a mathematical reduction; a constant adjustment of ingredients, seasoning and cooking times is needed for a proper reproduction of the original dishes. This can only be achieved by testing the recipes over and over again, which I did—by myself, with home economists and with home cooks. And of course, as in any fine restaurant, there will always be slight— very slight—variations in such matters as seasoning and the use of sauces.

The quantities of food in each serving in The Russian Tea Room Cookbook correspond as much as possible to the quantities served in the restaurant. And food is decorated and served as in The Tea Room.

The ingredients used in the recipes of this book are readily available in supermarkets and gourmet stores. With the exception of a few, such as caviar and salmon, they are not expensive. No special cooking equipment is needed. Nor are any special cooking techniques necessary besides those of a good home cook. The majority of the recipes are easy; a few require a little patience and practice for perfect results. All of the recipes in this book will enrich your cooking repertoire and enhance your reputation as a superb cook. Besides, re-creating them in your home will remind many of you of pleasant hours spent in the original home of these dishes, The Russian Tea Room. Remember that you don't have to travel far to learn a beautiful new cuisine—and that Russian food does not have to be prepared by Russian chefs!

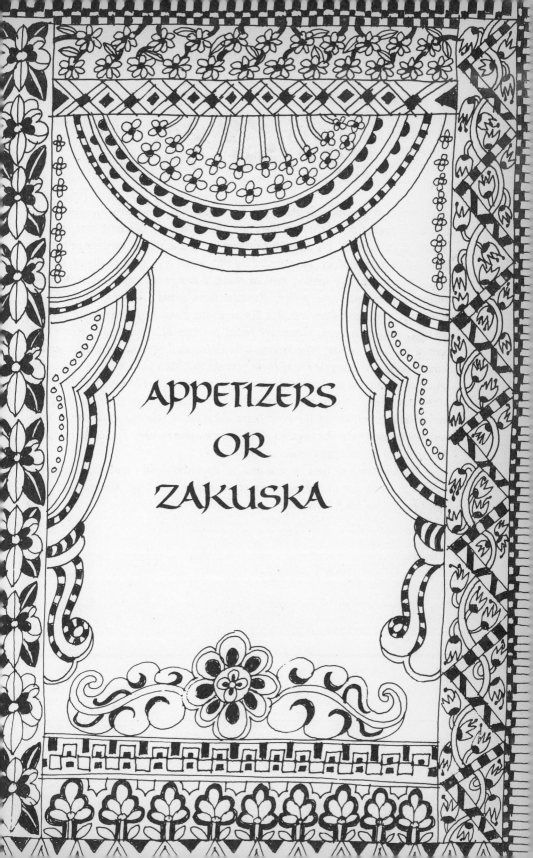

APPETIZERS
OR
ZAKUSKA

A glance at our menu will show you the richness of these hors d'oeuvres à la Russe. Supreme among all of them are the caviars of different varieties, as described on page 25. We serve our caviars in the traditional manner in a glass bowl set in a bowl of ice, surrounded by the classic accompaniments of minced egg yolks, minced egg whites, minced onion, a wedge of lemon and white toast points or for those who prefer, Russian black bread. A rewarding way of sampling other hors d'oeuvres à la Russe is our Zakuska Platter, with pickled herring, smoked salmon, miniature boiled potatoes filled with sour cream and topped with red caviar, Mushrooms à la Grecque, Eggplant Orientale, and a lemon wedge. Any single one of these zakuska will start your meal in style. But you may follow the lead of many of our guests, who want to have a light lunch or supper. They simply make a meal of their favorite appetizers, as does the master choreographer of the New York City Ballet, George Balanchine, who restores himself with the zakuska of his native country when he comes into The Russian Tea Room after the show.

The following recipes for cold and hot appetizers will enable you to start a meal à la Russe, or to integrate any of the dishes into your own menus. And don't forget the black bread and plenty of sweet butter!

Baked Salmon à la Russe

Russians love salmon, which is plentiful in their country.

Serves 12 as a zakuska

Serves 6 as main course servings

6 medium potatoes (about 2½ pounds)
5 tablespoons butter
2 large onions, chopped
10 ounces sliced smoked salmon (8 slices)
½ teaspoon salt (if the salmon is mild and not too salty itself)

¼ teaspoon freshly ground pepper
1 tablespoon minced fresh dill weed
3 eggs
2 cups light cream or half and half
4 teaspoons butter

Preheat the oven to low (325°F). Peel the potatoes. Slice them as thin as possible. Soak potatoes in cold water for 5 to 10 minutes. Drain and dry between paper towels. Heat 4 tablespoons of the butter in a large frying pan. Add the onions. Cook over medium heat, stirring constantly, for 3 to 5 minutes or until golden; do not brown. Butter an 8-cup baking dish with the remaining tablespoon of butter. Line the bottom with ⅓ of the potatoes. Sprinkle half the onions over the potatoes and top with half the salmon slices. Sprinkle salmon with a little of the salt, pepper and dill weed. Repeat the layers, ending with potatoes. Beat the eggs and cream together. Pour over the contents of the baking dish and dot with the 4 teaspoons of butter. Bake for about 1¼ hours, or until custard has set and a silver knife inserted in the middle of the baking dish tests clean. Serve immediately.

Salmon Roll

Serves 6

½ pound Nova Scotia or other cured salmon (end pieces are satisfactory)
½ pound cream cheese, at room temperature

¼ to ½ teaspoon dried dill weed
1 two-ounce jar pimiento-stuffed olives, drained

Grind the salmon fine in a food processor but do not liquefy; or put through the fine blade of a meat grinder. Combine ground salmon and cream cheese in a large bowl. Add the dill weed. With a wooden spoon, or preferably an electric mixer, blend thoroughly until the mixture is smooth. Transfer mixture to a large sheet of aluminum foil. Using a spatula, spread the mixture into a rectangle measuring 12 by 4 inches. Place drained olives lengthwise in a row in the center of the salmon mixture. Again with a spatula, bring the mixture over the olives, forming a closed roll measuring 12 inches in length. Turn the ends of the foil over the ends of the salmon roll and bring up the sides of the foil to enclose the salmon roll completely. Chill in the refrigerator for at least 6 hours or until firm enough to slice. To serve, peel aluminum foil carefully off the salmon roll. Cut into 24 half-inch slices. Allow 4 slices per serving. Place slices on 6 individual salad plates lined with lettuce leaves. Garnish with cherry tomato, sprigs of watercress, radish roses and spring onions.

Marinated Salmon

Serves 6 as zakuska

6 *medium-thick slices smoked salmon*	¼ *teaspoon black pepper*
2 *Bermuda onions cut in thin rings*	1 *bay leaf*
	⅓ *cup vinegar*
1 *small garlic clove, crushed*	¼ *cup olive oil*
½ *teaspoon salt*	½ *cup salad oil*

Place alternate layers of salmon and onion rings in a glass jar or ceramic crock. The jar should be no larger than necessary for the marinade to cover the fish. Combine the remaining ingredients and pour over the fish and onions. Close the container and store in the refrigerator for 7 to 10 days before using. You may juggle the amount of vinegar and oil to suit your own taste, increasing the vinegar for a more pickled taste. Arrange on a plate and serve with black bread.

Herring Salad

A fine zakuska and an asset to any buffet, Herring Salad is popular throughout Germany and Scandinavia as well as Russia.

Serves 6

3 *salt herrings (from Scandinavian specialty or gourmet shops)*
   half-milk, half-water to cover
1½ *cups cubed cooked beets*
½ *cup cubed cooked peeled potatoes*
2 *cups cubed cooked mixed cold meats (beef, pork, veal and/or tongue)*
2 *tart apples, cored but not peeled, cubed*
1 *large dill pickle, cubed*

2 *tablespoons capers, drained*
2 *hard-cooked eggs, chopped*
1 *teaspoon freshly ground pepper*
1 *cup heavy cream*
3 *tablespoons white vinegar*
1 *teaspoon prepared mustard*
½ *teaspoon salt*
1 *tablespoon sugar*
   salad greens as desired
3 *hard-cooked eggs*
1 *cup minced parsley*
1 *large radish rose*

Wash herrings and soak overnight in equal parts of milk and water to cover. Drain, dry and cut off tails and heads. Remove all bones and cut into ½-inch cubes. In a large, deep bowl combine herring, beets, potatoes, meats, apples, dill pickle, capers and chopped eggs. Season with pepper and mix thoroughly with a wooden spoon. Whip the cream in a small bowl. Stir in vinegar, mustard, salt and sugar and mix well. Add to the herring mixture and toss the salad lightly with a fork (preferably wooden). Line a round serving platter with salad greens. Pile the salad on the greens in the shape of a pyramid. Separate the yolks and whites of 2 of the hard-cooked eggs and cut the third egg into 8 lengthwise slices. Chop yolks, then whites, fine, keeping them separate. Surround salad with alternate mounds of chopped egg yolks, minced parsley and chopped egg whites. Arrange egg slices on top of the salad in the shape of a blossom and top with the radish rose. Serve immediately.

Russian Egg Salad

Serves 12 as a zakuska

Serves 4 to 6 as a salad

6 hard-cooked eggs	1 teaspoon water
½ teaspoon salt	1 cup mayonnaise
¼ teaspoon black pepper	¼ teaspoon minced garlic
1 teaspoon dry mustard	1 tablespoon finely minced spring
¼ teaspoon sugar	onions or chives

Cut the eggs into neat, thin rounds. Sprinkle with salt and pepper. Mix the mustard, sugar and water to a smooth paste. Mix it well with the mayonnaise and minced garlic. Fold the mayonnaise carefully into the sliced seasoned eggs. Do this gently with a wooden spoon, taking care not to break the egg slices. Place in an oval or rectangular bowl. Top with minced green onions or chives.

Chopped Chicken Liver

Good fresh chicken fat adds greatly to the flavor of chopped chicken liver. If it is not possible to buy rendered chicken fat, make your own. Cut all fat and skin from a 2-to-3-pound frying chicken (you'll need the larger size if the chicken is lean). Cut fat and skin into small pieces, place in a small, heavy frying pan or saucepan and cook very slowly over very low heat. Strain the hot fat through a fine strainer to remove the grieben *(cracklings) and use these when making biscuits, or as a sandwich filling. There should be approximately ½ cup of rendered chicken fat.*

Makes about 2 cups

½ pound chicken livers	2 hard-cooked eggs, cut into
½ cup chicken fat	quarters
2 medium onions, minced	1 teaspoon salt
	⅓ teaspoon freshly ground pepper

Wash the chicken livers by dipping them quickly into a bowl of cold water. Drain and dry between paper towels. If the livers are large, cut them into halves. Heat the chicken fat in a medium-heavy frying pan. Add the onions. Cook, stirring constantly for 3 to 5 minutes, until the onions are soft and golden; do not brown. With a slotted spoon transfer the onions to a chopping bowl or a food-processor bowl. Add the chicken livers to the frying pan. Cook, stirring all the time, over moderately high heat for 2 to 5 minutes, depending on size, or until livers are browned but still pink inside. Livers should be medium-rare; do not overcook. Add livers, pan juices, eggs, salt and pepper to the bowl containing the onions and mix well. Chop with a rounded chopper until fine. Or, if using a food processor, switch on and off 3 to 7 times, depending on the texture desired. Turn into a serving bowl, cover with foil or plastic wrap and refrigerate until needed. Return to room temperature before using. Serve with half of a hard-cooked egg on lettuce leaves for each plate.

Kholodetz

A SAVORY, COLD DISH FROM RUSSIA'S BALTIC COAST, OF GERMAN-SCANDINAVIAN ORIGIN. ALSO CALLED STUDEN.

Serves 6 to 8

2 *calf's feet (approximately 5 pounds)*
1 *large unpeeled Bermuda onion (1 pound)*
1 *large carrot*
2 *quarts cold water*

6 *whole black peppercorns*
3 *bay leaves*
1 *tablespoon salt*
1 *garlic clove, minced*
 vegetables for garnish

In a 6-quart soup kettle or saucepan, combine calf's feet, onion, carrot and water. Bring to the boiling point and skim thoroughly. Reduce heat to low and add peppercorns and bay leaves. Simmer covered for about 3 hours or until the calf's feet are tender. Transfer calf's feet and carrot to a bowl and cool. Strain broth through a fine sieve into a bowl. Chill for about 20 minutes and skim off any fat on the surface. Return to a clean soup kettle or saucepan and bring to the boiling point. Boil briskly without a cover for about 20 minutes or until broth is reduced to about 4 cups. Cool. Remove any fat that may have risen to the surface. With a small, sharp knife, cut off all the meat from the bones of the calf's feet. Cut meat into 1-inch strips. Cut the carrot into thin slices. Rinse a 2-quart mold with cold water. Arrange the carrot slices in concentric circles in the bottom of the mold. Place the mold into a pan partially filled with ice water. Spoon cooled stock over the carrots, a little at a time, until the carrot layer is partially covered but not floating. Place mold in the refrigerator and chill until set. Combine the meat strips, salt and garlic in a bowl and mix well. Turn into the mold, arranging over the jelled broth. Pour the remainder of the stock over it. Refrigerate and chill for 4 hours and longer or until the contents of the mold are firm to the touch. To serve, unmold onto a platter lined with salad greens, and decorate with watercress, cherry tomatoes, radish roses, black olives and bundles of 3 spring onions each, each wrapped in a carrot curl.

Grated Black Radishes

Serves 4

2 teaspoons minced onion	¼ teaspoon black pepper
2 black radishes, peeled	½ cup sour cream
1½ teaspoons salt	fresh lettuce leaves

Soak the onion in cold water for 15 minutes. Drain well. Grate the radishes into a bowl. Add the onion, salt and pepper. Toss with the sour cream and mound on lettuce leaves.

Mushrooms à la Grecque

Antoine Carème, the great early nineteenth-century French chef, introduced this dish to the St. Petersburg court when Czar Alexander I brought him to Russia. Russians have always been extremely fond of mushrooms and they have many varieties to choose from. To this day, urban and rural Russians take to the forest to gather the different varieties of wild mushroom, some of which are as large as a blin *(pancake). There is a mystical quality to this mushroom hunt, perhaps because of the Russians' deep ties to the forests that figure so prominently in their legends and literature.*

Serves 6 to 12

Serve chilled as a zakuska

1 cup dry white wine	½ teaspoon ground coriander
½ cup water	2 teaspoons salt
⅓ cup olive oil	1 teaspoon freshly ground pepper
¼ cup fresh lemon juice rind only (with as little of white membrane as possible) of 1 lemon, in 1 piece	3 medium onions, thickly sliced and separated into rings
3 bay leaves	2 pounds small white firm mushrooms
1 teaspoon dried thyme	salad greens, vegetables for garnish

Combine all the ingredients except the mushrooms in a large heavy saucepan. Bring to the boiling point. Cook, covered, over medium heat for 5 minutes. Add mushrooms. Cook, covered, over high heat (high heat keeps mushrooms light), stirring frequently with a wooden spoon, for 6 to 8 minutes or until mushrooms are tender but still firm. Turn into a china, glass or stainless-steel bowl. Cool. Cover with plastic wrap and chill thoroughly before serving. At serving time, drain mushrooms, remove bay leaves and lemon rind, leaving as many onion rings with the mushrooms as desired. Arrange on a serving dish lined with salad greens (or on individual plates lined with salad greens) and garnish with black and green olives, radish roses and 2 scallions for each serving. The spring onions may be tied with carrot curls.

Note: The mushrooms will keep for 2 to 3 weeks in a covered jar or dish in the refrigerator. The flavor improves after 2 or 3 days.

Eggplant Orientale

A DISH OF COLD CHOPPED EGGPLANT BAKED WITH
TOMATOES AND ONIONS, WITH A LIGHT AND SAVORY TASTE

Eggplant Orientale is an all-season RTR favorite. We serve it as a zakuska and recommend it also as a summer salad. Try Eggplant Orientale spread on dark pumpernickel or rolled in a crisp lettuce leaf, or as a dip for raw vegetables, especially long cucumber sticks.

Serves 12 as a zakuska

Serves 6 as salad

2 eggplants, each weighing
     approximately 1 pound
½ cup olive or salad oil
1 medium onion, minced
2 garlic cloves, minced
⅓ cup minced parsley
2 peppers, seeded, membranes
     removed, chopped fine
1 can (1 pound 12 ounces) Italian-
     style tomatoes, mashed
     (about 3½ cups)

3 tablespoons tomato paste
1 teaspoon dried basil
½ to 1 teaspoon dried oregano
¼ teaspoon ground coriander
1½ teaspoons salt
½ teaspoon freshly ground pepper
3 tablespoons tomato ketchup
3 tablespoons chili sauce
     lemon slices, vegetables for
     garnishing

Trim and peel eggplants. Cut them into 1-inch cubes. Turn eggplant cubes into a large oiled baking pan. Bake in an oven preheated to 350°F., stirring frequently, for about 45 minutes or until soft. While eggplant is baking, make the sauce. Heat the oil in a large (4-quart) heavy saucepan. Add onion, garlic and parsley. Cook over medium heat, stirring constantly, for about 5 to 7 minutes or until soft. Add peppers and cook for 3 more minutes. Add mashed tomatoes, tomato paste, basil, oregano, coriander and salt and pepper. Mix well. Cook covered over low heat, stirring frequently, for 20-30 minutes. Chop eggplant very fine or process in a food processor. Add chopped eggplant to tomato sauce and cook, covered, over low heat for 20 to 30 minutes more, stirring frequently. Remove from heat and cool. Then stir in ketchup and chili sauce and mix well. Check the seasoning and, if necessary, add more salt and pepper. Chill thoroughly. To serve, turn eggplant into a deep serving dish lined with salad greens, or on individual plates lined with a lettuce leaf. Garnish with carrot curls, cherry tomatoes, black olives, scallions and lemon slices.

Dolmas
(Stuffed Grapevine Leaves)

From the Middle East, where they appear on all tables, dolmas *found their way to the Russian zakuska table. They also make a delicious main course. Usually, ground meat is used in the making of hot dolmas, whereas cold dolmas are made without meat. However, either variety, served hot or cold, is excellent eating. The grapevine leaves used for dolmas may be either fresh or preserved in brine; the latter are far more commonly used. The leaves preserved in brine and bottled or packed in cans may be found in Greek and Oriental groceries and in gourmet shops. When using fresh grapevine leaves, try to have them all the same size. Blanch to soften them by plunging a few at a time into boiling water for 3 to 4 minutes; drain and dry them with paper towels. Cut off the stems. When using preserved grapevine leaves, remove some of their salt by putting them into a bowl and pouring boiling water over them to cover. Separate the leaves with two forks and let them soak in the hot water for 10 minutes. Drain, soak in cold water for 3 to 4 minutes, drain again and shake dry. If the leaves are very salty, repeat the procedure. If they are only lightly salted, soak them in cold water once, separating the leaves, for 3 to 4 minutes. Drain and shake each leaf dry. Since pickled grape leaves and blanched fresh grape leaves tear easily, and since a few leaves are likely to be unsightly, it is advisable to have 6 or more spare leaves on hand in case they are needed.*

Cold Rice-Stuffed Dolmas

At The Russian Tea Room we often serve these as an Easter dinner appetizer.

Makes about 45 dolmas

¾ cup olive oil
4 medium onions, chopped
1 cup long-grain rice
2 garlic cloves, crushed
½ cup fresh herbs (about 2
     tablespoons each parsley,
     mint, coriander, dill weed)
     stemmed and minced (save
     stems)
1 teaspoon cinnamon
4 tablespoons currants or chopped
     raisins

4 tablespoons pine nuts (pignoli)
1 teaspoon salt
¼ teaspoon freshly ground pepper
2 cups hot chicken bouillon or
     vegetable broth
½ cup fresh lemon juice
1 8-to-9-ounce jar pickled grape
     leaves, page 41 (or about
     45 fresh young grape
     leaves, stemmed and
     blanched)

Heat ½ cup of the olive oil in a large (10- to 12-inch) heavy frying pan. Add the onions and cook over medium heat, stirring constantly, for 3 to 5 minutes or until soft; do not brown. Add the rice and cook, stirring all the time, for 3 to 4 minutes. Add garlic, minced herbs, cinnamon, currants, pine nuts, salt and pepper, 1 cup bouillon and ¼ cup lemon juice. Simmer covered over low heat, stirring frequently, for about 5 minutes. Cool, but leave covered.

Place grape leaves on a clean, flat surface, shiny side down. Depending on the size of the leaves, place from 1 to 4 teaspoons of the cooled stuffing in the center of each leaf near the stem end. Fold the stem end over the filling. Fold sides toward the middle and roll up like a small cigar. Squeeze *very gently* in the palm of your hand to make the rolls hold together.

Lightly oil a baking dish measuring approximately 11 by 7 by 1½ inches. Cover the bottom of the pan with one layer of dolmas. Sprinkle dolmas with reserved herb stems; this adds flavor to the dish. Top with a layer of the remaining dolmas. Combine the remaining cup of hot bouillon, the remaining ¼ cup olive oil and the remaining ¼ cup lemon juice. Pour over the dolmas. Cover the pan loosely with aluminum foil. Top the foil with a pan or dish slightly smaller, pressing the pan snugly into the baking dish. This will keep the dolmas in place while cooking and prevent the stuffing from oozing out. Cook in a slow oven (preheated to 325°F.) for 1 hour. Turn oven off and keep dolmas in the closed oven for about 30 minutes. Chill before serving.

Hot Dolmas with Ground Lamb

Though ground beef or veal may be used in these dolmas, ground lamb makes by far the more flavorful dish.

Makes about 65 dolmas

2 tablespoons olive oil
1 pound lean ground lamb
2 large onions, chopped
2 garlic cloves, minced
½ cup long-grain rice
1 8-ounce can tomato sauce (1 cup)
½ cup water
1 teaspoon salt
¼ teaspoon freshly ground pepper
½ cup fresh herbs (about 2 tablespoons each parsley, mint, coriander, dill weed) stemmed and minced (save stems)
1-pound jar or can pickled grape leaves, prepared as on page 41 (or about 60 to 70 fresh grape leaves, stemmed and blanched)
1½ cups hot chicken bouillon or vegetable broth
½ cup fresh lemon juice

Heat olive oil in a large (10- to 12-inch) heavy frying pan. Add ground lamb, onions and garlic. Cook over medium-to-high heat, stirring constantly, for about 5 minutes, breaking up the lumps of meat. Add rice and, stirring all the time, cook for 3 to 5 minutes. Add tomato sauce, water, salt, pepper and herbs. Mix well. Simmer, covered, over medium heat, stirring frequently, for about 5 minutes. Cool but leave covered.

Place grape leaves on a clean, flat surface, shiny side down. Depending on the size of the leaves, place from 1 to 4 teaspoons of the cooled stuffing in the center of the leaf near the stem end. Fold the stem end over the filling. Fold sides toward the middle and roll up like a small cigar. Squeeze *very gently* in the palm of your hand to make the rolls hold together. Cover the bottom of a lightly oiled 3-quart casserole with 3 to 4 grape leaves. Layer the dolmas in the casserole, scattering the herb stems between layers. Combine bouillon and lemon juice and pour over dolmas. Cover with a small plate that fits inside the casserole to prevent them from coming undone, and top with a lid. Cook over low heat for 45 to 60 minutes. Remove from heat and let stand, covered, at room temperature for 15 to 20 minutes. Serve hot, preferably from the casserole.

Sweet-and-Sour Smelts

An easy way to remove the backbone and bones from smelts is to run a finger under the backbone and lift it up; the backbone and small bones attached will come off together.

Serves 6 to 8 as a zakuska

4 medium-size smelts, dressed,
    weighing approximately 1
    pound, or 4 mackerel
    fillets, weighing
    approximately 1 pound
¼ cup light cream or half and half
1 teaspoon dried tarragon leaves,
    crumbled
¼ cup flour
4 tablespoons cooking oil
2 medium onions, thinly sliced

2 medium carrots, thinly sliced
1 8-ounce can tomato sauce
½ cup water
1 bay leaf
2 whole cloves
1 teaspoon salt
2 teaspoons brown sugar
1 tablespoon vinegar
½ lemon, thinly sliced
    watercress or parsley for garnish

If you are using the smelts, leave them whole. If you are using mackerel fillets, cut each fillet into 4 pieces. Wash the fish quickly under running cold water and blot dry between paper towels. Pour the cream into a shallow bowl. Sprinkle the tarragon over the cream and let stand for 5 minutes. Put the flour into another shallow bowl, or on a plate. Dip each smelt or piece of mackerel in the cream and coat it with the flour on all sides, shaking off excess flour. Heat 3 tablespoons of the oil in a large frying pan. Add the fish in one layer, brown, turn, and brown the other side. Transfer the fish with a slotted spoon onto a deep platter. Add the remaining tablespoon of oil to the frying pan. Add the onions and cook, stirring constantly, for about 3 minutes or until golden. Add the carrot slices. Over low heat, stirring frequently, cook onions and carrots together for 5 to 10 minutes. Add the tomato sauce, water, bay leaf, cloves, salt, sugar, vinegar and lemon slices. Cover the frying pan and simmer over low heat for 15 minutes. Stir frequently. Allow mixture to cool; check the seasoning. Pour the cooled sauce over the fish. Chill. Garnish with parsley or watercress before serving.

Forshmak Dragomiroff

This is one of the hot zakuska dishes that also makes a fine light main lunch or supper dish in America. The word forshmak is derived from the German and translates as a "before taste," i.e., appetizer. As with all traditional dishes, there are as many versions of forshmak as there are cooks. Ours was given to The Russian Tea Room by the descendant of one of the Muscovite merchant princes, with the remark that nothing was ever wasted in her grandfather's kitchen.

Serves 6

2 cups water
¾ teaspoon salt
1 pound potatoes (3 medium or 4 small), peeled and cut into 1-inch cubes
3 tablespoons milk
4 tablespoons butter
1 small onion, minced
2 cups cooked ground ham (8 to 10 ounces, or an abundant ½ pound)

2 cups cooked ground roast beef (8 to 10 ounces, or an abundant ½ pound)
½ cup sour cream
⅓ cup minced herring party snacks in wine sauce, drained (about 7 pieces)
1 large dill pickle, minced, or more, to taste
1 cup grated Parmesan cheese
½ teaspoon freshly ground pepper
3 eggs, separated

In a small saucepan, combine water and ½ teaspoon of the salt and bring to the boiling point. Add the potatoes. Cover and cook over medium heat for about 10 minutes or until soft. Drain. Using a potato masher, mash the potatoes, or press them through a sieve; do not use a food processor. There should be about 2 cups of mashed potatoes. Beat in milk and 1 tablespoon of the butter. Heat 1 tablespoon of the remaining butter in a small frying pan. Add the onion and cook over medium heat, stirring constantly, for 3 to 5 minutes or until soft; do not brown. In a large bowl combine mashed potatoes, onion, ham, roast beef, sour cream, herring, pickle and ½ cup of the Parmesan. Season with remaining ¼ teaspoon of the salt and with the pepper. Add the egg yolks and mix thoroughly, using a wooden spoon. Beat the egg whites until stiff but not dry. Fold carefully into potato-meat mixture. Turn into a buttered shallow 2-quart baking dish. Dot with the remaining 2 tablespoons of butter and sprinkle with the remaining ½ cup of Parmesan. Bake in a preheated moderate oven (350°F.) for 25 to 30 minutes or until golden brown. Serve as is, or with Tomato Sauce (page 137) or Mushroom Sauce (page 132).

Circassian Chicken

COLD POACHED CHICKEN WITH WALNUT SAUCE

*The Circassians, known also as Cherkess, are an indigenous mountain
people of the western Caucasus, whose women were—and are—
known for their beauty. Their cooking, like all Caucasian cooking,
relies on their plentiful walnuts and other nuts and fruits, which are
frequently served with chicken (see Pressed Chicken Tabakà, page 78).
Circassian Chicken may be made from a cold roasted bird, but a moist
flavorful poached chicken is preferable and more usual. Circassian
Chicken may be served as a zakuska; it is also an excellent summer
main dish.*

Serves 12 as a zakuska

Serves 6 as a main course

1 *4½- to 5-pound stewing chicken*
1 *quart water*
2 *medium onions, peeled*
2 *carrots*

2 *celery stalks*
½ *cup parsley sprigs*
1 *teaspoon salt*
¼ *teaspoon Tabasco*

SAUCE:

2 *cups shelled walnuts (½ pound)*
3 *slices firm white bread (crusts trimmed off) cut into pieces*

1 *tablespoon minced onion (optional)*
2 *tablespoons (sweet Hungarian) paprika*

Remove the skin and all visible fat from the chicken. Place chicken
in a large soup kettle; add the water, the peeled onions, carrots, celery
stalks, parsley, salt and Tabasco. Bring to the boiling point and skim as
needed throughout cooking time. Lower heat and simmer, covered, for
about 1½ hours or until tender; do not overcook. If there is sufficient
time before serving, cool the chicken in its own broth. Strain the broth
and reserve 1¼ cups. (Save the remaining broth for soup.) Chill the 1¼
cups chicken broth and remove any fat that has risen to the surface. If
there is no time to chill the broth, remove as much fat as possible with a
spoon, or blot the fat up with double layers of paper towels.
Bone the cooled chicken and cut it into as many neat slices as

possible. Pull any bits and pieces off the bones and reserve them. Place the chicken slices neatly on a serving platter and scatter the chicken bits among them. Cover with plastic wrap and refrigerate. For the sauce, combine the walnuts, bread and optional minced onion in a blender or a food processor. Process until almost smooth. Add the 1¼ cups of chicken stock slowly to the mixture (in a processor, pour through the feed tube) and process again until well blended. There should be about 2½ cups of sauce. Spread the sauce over the chicken slices and pieces. Sprinkle with the paprika. Serve cool or chilled, with a tossed green salad.

Note: The paprika may also be blended into the sauce.

SOUPS WITH PIROJOK

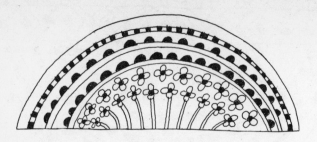

Ever since it opened its doors, The Russian Tea Room has been famous for the excellence of its soups—true to the Russian tradition that "soup is the meal." Indeed, many of our soups, rich with a diversity of vegetables and meats, such as the Borscht, the Roszolnik, the Okroshka, the Mushroom and Barley soup and the Potage Saint-Germain are substantial enough to be a light meal. They are served in large soup plates and a bowl of sour cream accompanies the soups that call for it. But all the soups, without exception, be they hot or cold, be it summer or winter, spring or fall, are served with a piping-hot, flaky pirojok stuffed with a savory meat filling (see page 62), made in our bakery.

A plate of soup, especially the Hot Borscht (favored by Leonard Bernstein), is the choice of many of our guests who drop in for supper after the theater or concert. A plate of soup is also a satisfying beginning to lunch, our guests tell us, some admitting that they cannot resist following it with one of our specialties, such as shashlik or Chicken Kiev.

At The Russian Tea Room we also offer the delicate, simply garnished consommés that Russians have always liked as meal starters. These we serve always with a pirojok.

Few dishes from another cuisine lend themselves as well to American food habits as Russian soups. They will warm us in winter and cool us in the summer. They are easy to prepare, they can be made yesterday and eaten today and tomorrow, when they will taste even better. Soup and salad become a festive lunch with one of The Russian Tea Room soups featured in the following recipes.

Hot Borscht

A BEET AND VEGETABLE SOUP

Borscht and Chicken Kiev are the most famous of all The Russian Tea Room favorites. There are as many borschts, it is said, as there are Russian grandmothers. Some, like the Ukrainian borscht, contain meat. The Russian Tea Room Borscht is the classic one, from Moscow, always served with sour cream and, of course, a pirojok. Russian peasants make a whole meal of their borscht, together with black bread, sweet butter and a glass of beer (in Russia, it would be a glass of kvass).

Years ago one of the Russian chefs at The RTR, Volodya Ribincoff, was interviewed by the food editor of a New York daily for our borscht recipe. "First take one hundred bones-es, forty beets-es—" "Wait!" she cried. "I want this recipe for six people!" "Can't make borscht for six people!" he bellowed, and she never got the recipe.

Serves 6

6 cups beef or chicken consommé, or 3 cups consommé and 3 cups Simple Kvass (see page 66)	¾ cup thinly sliced onions
	1 teaspoon sugar
	1½ cups julienne strips of raw beets
1 cup tomato sauce	salt and pepper, if needed
1½ cups shredded cabbage	2 teaspoons red-wine vinegar (optional)
¾ cups thinly sliced celery	¼ cup minced fresh dill weed
¾ cup shredded carrots	sour cream

Pour consommé into a large soup kettle. Add tomato sauce, cabbage, celery, carrots and onions. Bring to the boiling point and turn heat to low. Skim soup. Simmer, covered, for about 10 minutes or until vegetables are tender but still keep their shape. Skim as needed. Stir in sugar and add the beets. Simmer, covered, for 10 more minutes or until beets are tender. Check the seasonings; if necessary, add salt and pepper to taste. Stir in vinegar if you are using it. Turn soup into a tureen or 6 individual soup bowls and sprinkle with the dill. Serve hot, with sour cream on the side.

Cold Borscht

The traditional cold borscht season at The RTR begins on the first day of the baseball season in New York and ends the last day of the World Series—thus the cold borscht season is easy to remember! Our Cold Borscht is something else when we add iced vodka and serve it in a tall tea glass with holder, along with a long iced-tea spoon. The spoon serves to catch the soup's delicious little shreds of beet, cucumber and fresh dill.

Serves 6

7 to 8 cups chicken consommé
1 cup uncooked beets cut into
    julienne strips
2½ cups finely chopped uncooked
    beets
1 cup finely chopped carrots
1 cup finely chopped onions

1 tablespoon red-wine vinegar
    salt to taste
2 raw egg yolks
1 tablespoon sugar
1½ cups sour cream
2 tablespoons fresh lemon juice
1 cucumber, cut into ¼-inch dice
¼ cup minced fresh dill weed

Pour consommé into a large soup kettle except for 1 cup. Place this 1 cup of consommé in a small saucepan. Add the julienned beets and simmer, covered, over medium heat for about 10 minutes. Strain into kettle containing the larger amount of consommé. Reserve julienned beets. Bring consommé to the boiling point. Add chopped uncooked beets, carrots and onions and stir in the vinegar. Over medium heat, cook, covered, for 15 to 20 minutes or until vegetables are very soft. Strain into a bowl and discard vegetables. Chill broth thoroughly. In a soup tureen, beat together egg yolks, sugar, sour cream and lemon juice; the mixture must be smooth. Gradually stir in the chilled broth to make a smooth mixture. If lumpy, strain again. Chill for 15 to 20 minutes more. At serving time, add the reserved julienned beets and the cucumber and sprinkle with the dill.

Borshok

A RUBY-RED SOUP MADE FROM BEETS SIMMERED IN CONSOMMÉ

For parties, Borshok is served in cups, topped with a dollop of sour cream, with piroshki or with cheese-flavored croutons.

Serves 6

¾ pound beets (1 small bunch, or 3 medium or 4 to 5 small beets)
½ cup dry white wine or Simple Kvass (page 66)
½ cup water

7 to 8 cups beef or chicken consommé
salt
freshly ground pepper
2 teaspoons sugar (optional)

Trim and scrub the beets. Cook them in boiling water until tender. Drain and cool. Peel the beets and cut them either into thin slices or into ¼- to ½-inch dice. Place the beets in a bowl (not aluminum). Add the wine (or kvass) and the water. There should be enough liquid to cover the beets; if not, add a little more water. Let the beets stand at room temperature for 2 to 3 hours or cover with plastic wrap and refrigerate overnight. At serving time, heat the consommé and add the beets, together with their liquid, salt and pepper to taste and the sugar if you are using it. Cook, covered, over low to medium heat for 5 to 10 minutes. Strain the soup into a soup tureen or into cups and top each serving with 2 to 3 teaspoons sour cream. Serve hot.

Note: For a richer, though not a traditional, flavor, do not strain the soup but serve with the beets, topped with sour cream.

Green Schi

SPINACH SOUP, DELICIOUS BOTH HOT AND COLD

In Russia, Green Schi is usually made with sorrel or nettles rather than spinach. However, spinach or any leafy green vegetable makes a fine soup. It is enhanced by being served cold the next day.

Serves 6

1½ pounds fresh spinach or 2 ten-
    ounce packages chopped
    frozen spinach, thawed
  5 tablespoons butter
⅓ cup minced onion
  5 tablespoons flour
  5 cups chicken bouillon

2 cups heavy cream
1 teaspoon salt
½ teaspoon freshly ground pepper
1 to 2 hard-cooked eggs, thinly
    sliced
3 tablespoons minced fresh dill
    weed

Cut roots and any thick stems from the fresh spinach. Wash in several changes of cold water, drain and pat dry between paper towels. Mince spinach, if you are using the fresh, preferably in a food processor. It is not necessary to further mince the chopped, frozen spinach. Heat butter in a large heavy saucepan. Add onion and cook, stirring constantly, for 3 to 5 minutes or until soft; do not brown. Stir in flour and blend well. Cook over medium heat, stirring constantly, for 2 to 3 minutes or until flour is beginning to turn golden—no more. Add chicken bouillon and mix well. Add minced spinach and blend. Reduce heat and cook for about 5 minutes, stirring constantly. Stir in cream, salt and pepper. Cook without a cover over low heat, stirring frequently, for 3 to 5 minutes or until thoroughly heated through. Do not boil. Turn into a tureen and float egg slices on top. Sprinkle with dill before serving. Serve hot. Or, if a cold soup is desired, chill before adding egg slices and dill, and add these just before serving.

Roszolnick à la Russian Tea Room

A favorite of many of our guests who like the tantalizing combination of flavors, Roszolnick is perfect Sunday lunch fare on a cold winter's day.

Serves 6

1 *pound chicken wings*
1 *pound chicken necks*
1 *pound chicken giblets*
1 *large carrot, thinly sliced*
4 *medium potatoes (approximately ½ pound) thinly sliced*
2 *stalks celery, diced*
1 *medium-sized onion, chopped*

1 *large bay leaf*
1 *teaspoon salt*
½ *teaspoon freshly ground pepper*
7 *cups chicken bouillon or water*
2 *cups light cream or half and half*
1 *large dill pickle, seeded and cut into ¼-inch cubes*
¼ *cup sour cream*

Cut off wing tips and discard. Skin chicken necks and cut into halves. Remove any fat from the giblets. In a large soup kettle, combine chicken wings, necks and giblets. Add carrot, potatoes, celery, onion, bay leaf, salt, pepper and bouillon or water. Bring to the boiling point and skim. Reduce heat to low. Simmer, covered, for about 1½ to 2 hours. Skim frequently, removing scum and fat that has risen to the surface of the soup. Stir in light cream (or half and half) and sour cream and heat through. At serving time, stir in dill pickle. If desired, remove chicken necks and wings before serving.

Okroshka

A CHILLED MEAT AND VEGETABLE SOUP

*One of the triumphs of a trip to Russia was being introduced to
Okroshka in Leningrad at one of the classic hotel dining rooms. It is
exciting to find such a new combination of tastes, especially the
inclusion of kvass and scallions.*

Serves 6

4 hard-cooked eggs
1 cup sour cream
2 teaspoons prepared mustard,
      preferably Dijon
1 teaspoon sugar
1½ teaspoons salt
½ teaspoon freshly ground pepper
4 cups beef bouillon
1½ cups Kvass (page 64) or very
      stale beer (1 twelve-ounce
      can)
1 medium cucumber, peeled,
      seeded and cut into ¼-inch
      dice

1 medium dill pickle, drained and
      cut into ¼-inch dice
½ pound (about 1½ cups) cooked
      meats (boiled tongue, beef,
      preferably boiled, kielbasi
      and/or veal), cut into ¼-
      inch dice
¼ cup thinly sliced scallions, white
      and green part (about 3
      small)
3 tablespoons minced parsley or
      fresh dill weed

With a large spoon, mash eggs through a fine sieve into a large
bowl. Reserve about ¼ cup of the sieved eggs. Into the remaining eggs,
stir the sour cream, mustard, sugar, salt and pepper and mix well.
Gradually add the beef bouillon, stirring all the time, and then stir in
the Kvass or beer. Mix thoroughly; the consistency should be that of
half and half. Add the cucumber, dill pickle, meat and spring onions.
Stir to blend. Chill thoroughly for 2 to 3 hours. Check the seasoning; if
necessary, add salt and pepper to taste. At serving time, sprinkle with
the reserved sieved eggs and parsley or dill. Serve in chilled soup
bowls.

Oukha

This is a delicate, clear fish soup, traditionally made with Russia's abundant freshwater fish. However, the soup will also be delicious when made with saltwater fish, which is so much easier to obtain in many parts of America. The soup has a richer flavor if made with several varieties. Be sure to use firm, white-fleshed fish.

Serves 6

3 pounds mixed fish (cod, haddock, sea trout, bass, etc.)
1 large onion, chopped
1 leek, white and pale-green parts, chopped (about 1 cup)
4 parsley sprigs
1 celery stalk, chopped

1 bay leaf
1 teaspoon salt
12 peppercorns
2 quarts water
½ cup dry white wine
2 tablespoons minced fresh dill weed

Trim off the meaty parts of about half of the fish and reserve. Put the remaining fish, the trimmings and all the other ingredients except the minced dill into a large soup kettle. Bring quickly to the boiling point, skim and lower the heat to very low. Simmer covered for 45 minutes, skimming as needed. Turn off heat and let stand covered for about 45 more minutes. Cut the reserved meaty parts of the fish into 1-inch pieces. Remove any skin and bones. Strain the fish broth into another saucepan. Discard trimmings. Bring broth to the boiling point and lower the heat. Add the reserved fish pieces and simmer covered for about 5 to 8 minutes or until the fish is tender but still firm; the cooking time depends on the thickness of the fish. Turn into a tureen and sprinkle with the dill. Ladle broth and pieces of fish into each individual soup plate or bowl. Serve with Kulebiaka (page 98).

Consommé Julienne

All our consommés are a perfect introduction to a substantial meal.

Serves 6

8 cups chicken consommé
1 cup celery in julienne strips,
    blanched
1 cup carrot in julienne strips,
    blanched

1 cup onion, thin round slices,
    blanched
  salt
  freshly ground pepper
1 tablespoon minced parsley

In a large saucepan, bring consommé to the boiling point. Add blanched vegetables. Simmer for 5 minutes or until vegetables are tender but still crisp. Check the seasoning; if necessary, add salt and pepper to taste. Sprinkle with parsley and serve hot.

Julienne is a way of cutting vegetables into long, thin, narrow strips. First cut the vegetables into thin slices measuring 1/16 to 1/8 inch. Stack the slices on top of each other and cut into 2- to 3-inch strips.

TO BLANCH VEGETABLES

Blanch each variety separately. Place vegetable to be blanched in a saucepan. Add enough boiling water to cover. Cook without a cover over medium heat for 3 minutes. Drain immediately.

Consommé Patti

Serves 6

8 cups chicken consommé
1/4 cup uncooked long-grain rice
1/2 cup carrot in julienne strips

  salt
  freshly ground pepper
1 tablespoon minced parsley

In a large saucepan, bring consommé to the boiling point. Add rice. Simmer for about 10 minutes or until almost tender. Add carrots. Cook 5 more minutes or until tender. Check the seasoning; if necessary, add salt and pepper to taste. Sprinkle with parsley and serve hot.

Consommé with Egg Noodles

Serves 6

8 *cups chicken or beef consommé*   *freshly ground pepper*
1 *cup fine egg noodles*   1 *tablespoon minced parsley*
   salt

In a large saucepan, bring consommé to the boiling point. Add egg noodles. Simmer without a cover for 10 minutes or until noodles are tender. Check the seasoning; if necessary, add salt and pepper to taste. Sprinkle with parsley and serve hot.

Chicken Consommé with Rice

Serves 6

8 *cups chicken consommé*   *freshly ground pepper*
⅓ *cup uncooked long-grain rice*   1 *tablespoon minced parsley*
   salt

In a large saucepan, bring consommé to the boiling point. Add rice. Simmer without a cover for 10 to 12 minutes or until tender. Check the seasoning; if necessary, add salt and pepper to taste. Sprinkle with parsley and serve hot.

Mushroom and Barley Soup

A WARMING AND SOOTHING SOUP FOR YOUNG AND OLD

Serves 6

2 tablespoons cooking oil
2 tablespoons butter
½ cup pearl barley
2 medium onions, thinly sliced
½ pound mushrooms, thinly sliced
8 cups chicken bouillon

1 large carrot, thinly sliced
1 teaspoon salt
¼ teaspoon freshly ground pepper
⅓ cup sour cream (optional)
2 tablespoons minced parsley or
      fresh dill weed

Heat the oil and butter in a large soup kettle. Add the barley and the onions and cook over medium heat, stirring constantly, for 3 to 5 minutes. Add mushrooms and cook for 4 to 5 minutes longer, or until the mushroom liquid has evaporated. Add chicken bouillon, carrot, salt and pepper. Bring to the boiling point and skim. Reduce heat to low and simmer, covered, for about 1 hour, stirring frequently. Remove from heat and stir in sour cream. Sprinkle with parsley or dill before serving.

Potage Saint-Germain
(Green Pea Soup)

Serves 6 to 8

1 pound dried green split peas
      (2½ cups)
10 cups water
½ cup chopped onions
½ cup chopped carrots
½ cup chopped celery
½ cup chopped leeks
1 bay leaf

1 ham bone
    salt
    freshly ground pepper
1 tablespoon flour (optional)
1 tablespoon butter, at room
      temperature (optional)
¼ cup minced parsley

Wash the peas under running cold water and pick out any foreign particles. Place the peas in a large soup kettle, add the water and cover. Soak the peas overnight; or bring to the boiling point and boil for 2 minutes, remove from heat, cover and let stand for 1 hour. (If the peas are the quick-cooking variety, there will be no need to soak or preboil them.) Add the onions, carrots, celery, leeks, bay leaf and ham bone. Bring to the boiling point and turn heat to low. Skim any foam from the top of the soup. Cover and simmer for 1½ to 2 hours or until the peas are falling apart and the meat separates from the ham bone. Skim frequently, as necessary. Remove from heat and take out the ham bone. Cut any meat off the bone, shred and reserve it. Discard the ham bone and bay leaf. Strain the soup through a sieve or purée in a food processor or a blender. Return soup to kettle and heat through. Check the seasonings; if necessary, add salt and pepper to taste. If the soup is too thin for your liking, knead together the flour and the butter; drop in pea-sized pieces into the soup, stirring constantly until absorbed. Cook over medium heat for 3 more minutes or until very hot. Add parsley just before serving.

Piroshki

These little meat-filled turnovers, usually served with soup, are among the delights of Russian cuisine. Served with our Borscht, in the traditional manner, they are all-time Russian Tea Room favorites. Our piroshki are made with puff paste—the elegant way of making them. But Russians also use Sour Cream Dough (below) which is quick and easy and also makes tasty piroshki. The word Pir *in Russian means feast, thus* pirog *(plural,* pirogi*) and* pirojok *(plural,* piroshki*) are two versions of a versatile pastry with many uses and many kinds of fillings. Our chief baker Denis Candela makes hundreds of these each day.*

Makes 18 4-inch pastries

MEAT FILLING

¼ *cup butter*
1 *medium onion, minced*
1 *pound round of beef, ground 3 or 4 times*
2 *tablespoons minced parsley*

1 *teaspoon salt*
¼ *teaspoon freshly ground pepper*
4 *drops Tabasco*
2 *eggs, well beaten*

To make the filling, heat the butter in a large, heavy frying pan. Add the onion and cook, stirring constantly, for 3 to 4 minutes or until golden; do not brown. Add the meat. Cook over medium heat, stirring constantly with a fork to loosen the meat, for 10 to 12 minutes or until the meat is brown and crumbly. Drain off excess fat. Add parsley, salt, pepper, Tabasco and eggs. Mix well. Turn the mixture into a bowl and chill. Remove any fat from the surface of the chilled meat.

SOUR CREAM DOUGH

3½ *cups sifted all-purpose flour (14 ounces)*
1 *teaspoon baking powder*

½ *cup salted butter*
2 *eggs, beaten*
1 *cup (½ pint) sour cream*

Sift together flour and baking powder into a large bowl. With a pastry cutter or two knives, cut in butter until the mixture resembles coarse cornmeal. Stir in eggs and sour cream. With your hands, knead dough lightly on a floured working surface until the mixture forms a smooth ball. Wrap dough in waxed paper or plastic wrap and refrigerate for 2 to 4 hours or until chilled but not frozen.

On a well-floured working surface, roll out the Sour Cream Dough (or the Puff Pastry, page 210) to the thickness of ⅛ inch. Using a glass or a cookie cutter, cut the dough into 5-inch rounds. Reroll the trimmings and keep on rerolling and cutting until you have 18 rounds, each measuring 5 inches in diameter. Place about 2 tablespoons of the filling on each round. Using a pastry brush or your finger, brush the edges of the rounds with a little beaten egg; this will help keep the edges together. Fold the dough over the filling and shape it into half moons. Press the edges firmly together to prevent filling from oozing out during baking. Place the filled piroshki on ungreased cookie sheets. Brush tops with beaten egg. Chill for 1 hour in the refrigerator. Preheat the oven to hot (400°F.). Bake piroshki for 25 to 30 minutes or until golden brown. Serve hot or cold, but preferably hot.

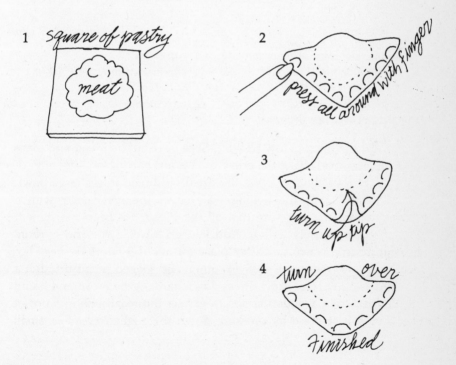

1 square of pastry
meat

2 press all around with finger

3 turn up tip

4 turn over
Finished

Kvass

Kvass is a pleasantly acid and mildly alcoholic beverage brewed from black bread fermented with yeast. Kvass is as Russian as a drink can be; in Russia it is drunk cold, as we drink soda, or used in soups, as in Okroshka (page 56). Kvass originated with the peasants, when they doused bread that had become too old and hard to eat with boiling water and allowed it to ferment for a few hours; it was then sweetened with honey, sugar and fruit—an inexpensive, easy drink, which also could be bottled for further use. The raisins in the kvass are said to help the clarification of the drink. Homemade kvass is a little effervescent and on the tart side. Kvass is sold in the streets from tank trucks, from which it is dispensed in cups. But non-Russians do not seem to take to it as a beverage, as I remember from my Russian trips. Bottled kvass stood on every restaurant dinner table, along with mineral water, but was passed over, by foreigners, in favor of beer or cider, to which it is similar and which can be substituted for it in Russian recipes.

Makes 6 to 7 cups

1 pound stale black bread or dark pumpernickel (darkest possible bread)	1 cup sugar
	¼ cup lukewarm water (110 to 115°F.)
4 quarts water (16 cups)	2 tablespoons raisins
2 tablespoons active dry yeast	

Preheat the oven to low (200°F.). Slice or chop the bread and place it on a baking sheet. Bake the bread for 1 hour, stirring occasionally, or until it is thoroughly dry. Place the dried-out bread into a large bowl. Boil the water; pour the boiling water over the bread. Stir with a wooden spoon, making sure that all the bread has been moistened. Cover the bowl loosely with a clean kitchen towel. Let stand at room temperature in a warm draft-free place for about 8 hours (in very hot weather, 4 to 6 hours will suffice). Strain the soaked bread through a sieve into another large bowl. Press down hard on the bread and liquid with the back of a wooden spoon to extract the maximum amount of juice; this is best done by pressing down the soaked bread in small batches. Discard the squeezed-out bread. Pour the ¼ cup of lukewarm water into a small bowl. Sprinkle the yeast and ½ teaspoon of the sugar over it. Stir to dissolve. Set the mixture in a warm, draft-free place (such as an unlighted oven) for about 10 minutes, or until it foams and is almost doubled in volume. Add the yeast mixture and the remaining sugar to the strained bread water and mix well. Cover with a towel and stand in a warm, draft-free place for 8 to 10 hours.

Strain the mixture again through a fine sieve or a triple layer of cheesecloth. Using a funnel, put the strained mixture into 2 or 3 quart bottles, filling each bottle two-thirds full. Divide the raisins between the bottles and drop them into each one. Cover each bottle top with plastic wrap and secure it with a rubber band. Let stand in a cool place for 3 to 5 days, or until the raisins have risen to the top and the sediment has dropped to the bottom of the bottle. Do not refrigerate. Decant the clear golden kvass into clean bottles, leaving behind all the sediment. (The Russians do not use the raisins, but discard them with the sediment.) Refrigerate until ready to use. but if the kvass is cloudy, strain it again through a fine sieve or a triple layer of cheesecloth. Use as a drink or in cold soups.

Note: If the kvass is to be used immediately as a drink, add 3 tablespoons of fresh mint leaves or 1 tablespoon of dried crumbled mint to it when adding the sugar. If the kvass is to be kept for any length of time, sterilize the bottles into which the final strained liquid is poured. Soak corks in boiling water before corking the bottles very tightly, and tie the corks down with strings running down the sides of the bottle to prevent the corks from popping.

Simple Kvass for Borscht

Simple kvass is not for drinking; it is used for cooking borscht. It gives flavor to the soup, and thanks to the beets in it, color.

Makes 4 to 5 cups

1 *pound stale black bread or dark pumpernickel (darkest possible bread)*

3 *quarts boiling water (12 cups)*
6 *large raw beets, peeled and thinly sliced*

Cut the bread into pieces and place it in a large bowl. Add the water and the beets, and mix well. Cover with a towel and set in a warm place for 2 to 3 days or until the mixture ferments. Strain bread mixture and liquid through a triple layer of cheesecloth or a fine sieve before using, pressing down hard on the bread with a wooden spoon to extract as much liquid as possible. Discard the bread mixture. The kvass should have a pleasant, acid taste. If you find it too strong for the soup, simply dilute it with water.

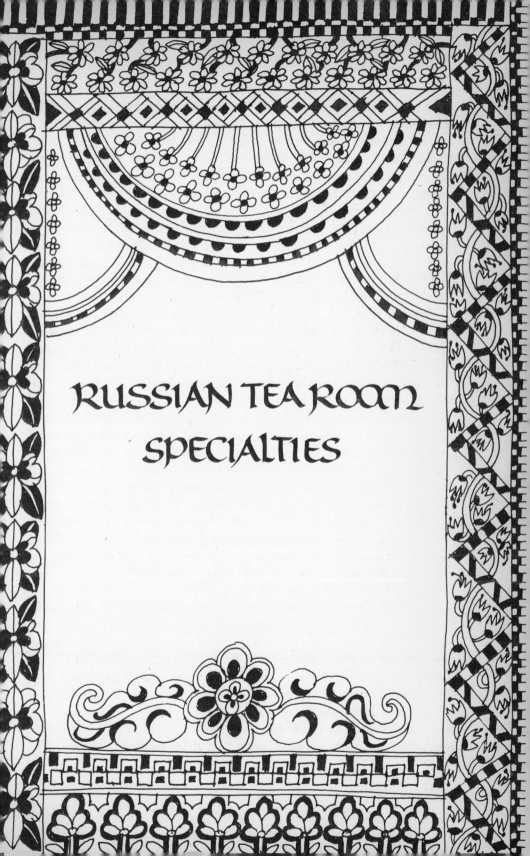

RUSSIAN TEA ROOM SPECIALTIES

Here are the recipes for the Russian specialties that have made The Russian Tea Room famous throughout the world. No one tells it better than the late Sol Hurok, the famed impresario who brought all the great Russian artists to the United States. Once, while in Moscow—Sol Hurok told us—he knew an American who was frantic for a good Russian meal. As the American was sitting in a restaurant, he could not help overhearing a conversation at the next table where a woman was telling her companion with great enthusiasm, "The borscht is great! The blini are out of this world! The Chicken Kiev is so wonderful that . . ." The American, no longer able to contain himself, rushed over to the next table. "Where can I find this great food?" he asked the two ladies. "Oh," they said, "we were talking about The Russian Tea Room in New York!" "Ah," said Mr. Hurok, "So true, so true."

As you know from having enjoyed them at The Russian Tea Room, or as you will learn as you read about them in the following recipes, our Russian specialties are extremely versatile. They are easy to fit into any menu of your own, whether it's an all Russian one with dishes from other sections of this book, or an American-Russian combination, also with recipes from this book. At The Russian Tea Room, for example, many of our guests, who might be planning to enjoy a Russian entrée, start the meal with one of the fresh fruits listed on the menu rather than a Russian soup. Or they might follow a zakuska or a Russian soup with all-American lamb or veal chops, also on our menu. If they dined on Kulebiaka, they might not wish for a pastry as a dessert, but would prefer to end the meal à la Russe with a glass of our own tea served with cherry preserves. The number of combinations for meals that are entirely Russian or a combination of Russian and American dishes is considerable and planned well enough to suit any appetite, any occasion, any season, and any amount of time needed to prepare a meal. Making your own menus from the recipes in this book is truly creative because they then will be your own creations. Besides, it is enormous fun!

And don't be tied down to one way of serving our specialties. If you want to use a certain sauce with a certain dish—even if this sauce is not the one served at The Russian Tea Room with that dish—try it! All year round we use fresh vegetables, and serve them as crisp, buttered accompaniments. You, of course, will serve the vegetables you like, just as you may prefer rice to kasha, or vice versa, or to stick to potatoes. The choice is up to you—just the way you accessorize a costume according to your mood.

All we wish is for you to make these Russian specialties your own and to enjoy them at home as you would enjoy them at The Russian Tea Room.

Shashlik Caucasian

MARINATED LEG OF SPRING LAMB, BROILED ON SKEWERS, WITH TOMATOES, GREEN PEPPER AND ONIONS.

The Tartars brought Shashlik (kebab) to Russia. Like the other Mongol tribes, they traveled with their tents and animals and cooked over open barbecues on skewers in the ancient tradition. Shashlik is one of our all-time favorites.

Serves 6

3 pounds boneless leg or shoulder of lamb
1 cup salad oil
½ cup fresh lemon juice
1 teaspoon salt
1 teaspoon freshly ground pepper
2 garlic cloves, crushed
2 large bay leaves
1½ teaspoons dried dill weed or 2 tablespoons chopped fresh dill weed

3 medium-size ripe but firm tomatoes, cut into halves (about 1¾ pounds)
3 medium-size peppers, seeded, membranes removed and cut into halves
3 small-to-medium-size onions, cut into halves

Cut all fat and gristle from the lamb. Cut the lamb into twelve 2-inch cubes. Make 2 or 3 small incisions in each lamb cube to prevent puckering during cooking. In a large bowl (do not use aluminum) combine oil, lemon juice, salt, pepper, garlic, bay leaves and dill. Mix thoroughly. Add lamb cubes and toss with a wooden spoon to coat them evenly with the marinade. Cover and refrigerate for 8 hours or overnight, turning lamb cubes 2 or 3 times for thorough marinating. Drain and reserve marinade. On each of six 12-inch skewers, thread 1 lamb cube, 1 tomato half, 1 pepper half, 1 onion half and 1 lamb cube. Arrange skewers on a large broiling rack. Brush with reserve marinade. Broil about 4 inches from heat source as follows:

    5 to 10 minutes for rare
    10 to 12 minutes for medium
    15 minutes for well done

Turn kebabs 2 or 3 times to cook evenly and brush frequently with the reserved marinade. At the table, slide the meat and vegetables off the skewers and onto a bed of hot, cooked rice or serve with Rice Pilaff (p. 125) if you prefer. Serve with Red Cabbage Relish (p. 72) and Madeira Sauce (p. 132).

Karsky Shashlik

MARINATED LAMB FILLET, LOIN AND KIDNEY GRILLED ON SKEWERS

This is the noblest and most wonderful of all shashliks. It is preferred by, among others, Paul Newman, Liza Minnelli, Anthony Quinn, José Ferrer and Woody Allen. If you have a cooperative butcher, ask him to remove all fat from a boned loin of lamb and its kidneys, and then cut the loin into 2 halves and cut these halves again into 2 pieces—there must be 4 pieces altogether. The tenderloins must also be halved and then halved again to make 4 pieces. Finally, cut 2 lamb kidneys into halves and trim off all the membranes and tubes.

Serves 4

MARINADE

1 cup salad oil
½ cup fresh lemon juice
1 teaspoon salt
1 teaspoon freshly ground pepper
2 garlic cloves, crushed

2 large bay leaves
1½ teaspoons dried dill or 2 tablespoons chopped fresh dillweed

---

4 pieces loin of lamb, trimmed of all fat and gristle
4 pieces fillet of lamb, trimmed of all fat and gristle

2 lamb kidneys, cut into halves and trimmed

Combine all the marinade ingredients in a large bowl; do not use aluminum. Mix thoroughly. Make a small incision on both sides of each loin and fillet piece to prevent puckering during cooking. Add the lamb (but not the kidneys) to the marinade and toss with a wooden spoon to coat pieces evenly with the marinade. Cover and refrigerate for 8 hours or overnight, turning 2 or 3 times for thorough marinating. Drain and reserve marinade. On each of 4 sixteen-inch skewers thread 1 piece of loin, 1 piece of fillet and ½ kidney. Arrange on a large broiling rack. Brush with reserved marinade. Broil about 4 inches from heat source as follows:

10 to 12 minutes for rare
15 to 20 minutes for medium
20 to 25 minutes for well done

Turn skewers frequently to allow shashlik to cook evenly. Brush frequently with the reserved marinade.

Serve with Red Cabbage Relish (page 72), Rice Pilaff (page 125) and Madeira Sauce (page 132).

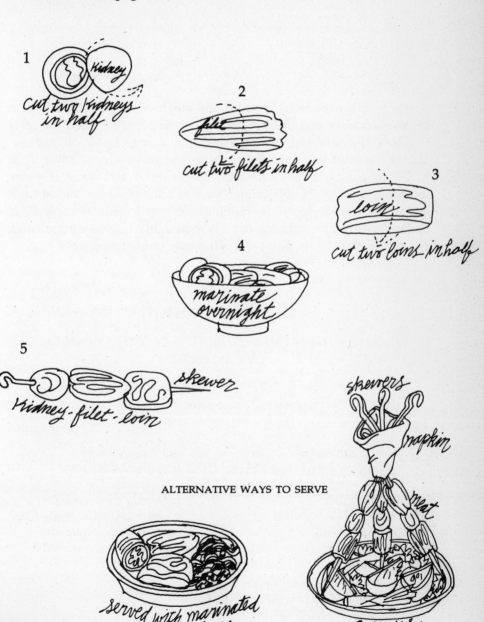

1 *cut two kidneys in half*

2 *cut two filets in half*

3 *cut two loins in half*

4 *marinate overnight*

5 *kidney-filet-loin* *skewer*

skewers
napkin
meat

ALTERNATIVE WAYS TO SERVE

served with marinated red cabbage

garnish

Red Cabbage Relish

Sour salt (citric acid) is available in supermarkets and in drug stores.

Makes about 4 cups

1 *one-pound head red cabbage*
1 *tablespoon sour salt*
1 *quart cold water*
1 *cup applesauce*

1 *tablespoon prepared mustard,*
     preferably Dijon
   salt
   freshly ground pepper

Trim the cabbage and remove any tough outer leaves. Cut it into quarters, remove and discard the hard stem part and shred the rest. Combine the sour salt and cold water in a large bowl; do not use aluminum. Add the shredded cabbage; the water should cover it. If not, add a little more water. Cover the bowl and soak at room temperature or in the refrigerator for 6 to 8 hours. Drain the cabbage and rinse it thoroughly under running cold water. Combine applesauce and mustard, add to cabbage and mix thoroughly. Season with salt and pepper to taste. Cover again and refrigerate until serving time.

Beef Stroganoff

LEAN BEEF WITH FRESH MUSHROOMS IN SOUR CREAM SAUCE EN CASSEROLE

A nineteenth-century dish created for Count Stroganoff, a dignitary at the court of Alexander III and a noted gourmet.

Serves 4 to 6

2 *pounds lean boneless sirloin or*
     bottom round, in one piece,
     trimmed of fat and gristle
2 *teaspoons salt*
½ *teaspoon freshly ground pepper*
4 *tablespoons butter*
1 *medium onion, thinly sliced*
1 *tablespoon flour*
1 *teaspoon powdered yellow*
     mustard or 1 tablespoon
     prepared Dijon-type

½ *cup dry white wine*
2 *teaspoons tomato paste*
     (optional)
1 *tablespoon minced onion*
½ *pound mushrooms, thinly sliced*
2 *tablespoons dry white wine*
1 *cup sour cream, preferably*
     warmed

Cut the meat into ½-inch-thick slices. Place between 2 sheets of waxed paper. Pound with a mallet or a heavy plate until meat is ¼ inch thick. Be careful not to tear meat. Cut meat into 2- by ½-inch slices. Place slices in one layer on a large platter. Sprinkle with salt and pepper and let stand at room temperature for 15 minutes. Heat 2 tablespoons of the butter in a deep, heavy frying pan or shallow saucepan large enough to hold all the ingredients. Add the sliced onion and cook over medium heat, stirring constantly, for about 5 minutes or until beginning to soften. Add meat to the pan. Cook for 3 minutes, turning beef slices constantly so that they are evenly browned on all sides. Stir in flour and mustard and cook, stirring constantly, for 1 more minute. Add the ½ cup of wine and optional tomato paste. Reduce heat to low, cover pan and simmer for 5 to 10 minutes, stirring frequently. In another frying pan, heat the remaining 2 tablespoons of butter. Add the minced onion and the mushrooms. Cook over medium heat for 2 minutes, add the 2 tablespoons of wine and cook for 2 more minutes; mushrooms should still be firm. Add mushrooms and their liquid to pan containing the meat. Check seasoning and stir in sour cream. Over lowest possible heat, simmer for about 5 minutes to heat dish through. Do not boil. Serve over a bed of hot cooked rice or kasha, with a green vegetable on the side.

Chicken Kiev (Cotelette à la Kiev)

*BONED BREAST OF CHICKEN STUFFED WITH BUTTER, BREADED
AND DEEP-FRIED TO A GOLDEN BROWN*

*This most famous and best known of all Russian dishes, as prepared in
The Russian Tea Room in the classic way, is generally acclaimed to be
The Best. Its Kievian origins are obscure and it seems most likely that
Chicken Kiev was a creation of the great French Chef Carême at the
Court of Alexander I. The sign of a properly prepared Chicken Kiev is
a spurt of butter at the first touch of the knife and fork. Our waiters
will do this first touch for you because the spurt of hot butter is so
unexpected.(When you do it at home, plunge the knife into the top of
the chicken gently and slide it straight down to the end of the bird.)*

Serves 6, 1 cutlet each

The boneless chicken breasts sold in almost all supermarkets
cannot be used for this dish because of their small size. And super-
market chicken quarters, from which a breast with the attached wing
bone necessary for this dish may be obtained, are almost always too
small after boning. For a perfect Russian Tea Room Chicken Kiev, ask
your butcher to cut the breasts from three 3½ pound chickens, and to
leave the wing bones attached to the breasts. One whole boned,
skinned and trimmed chicken breast, with 2 wing bones attached,
should weigh approximately 8 ounces (½ pound). Or each halved
chicken breast, boned, skinned and trimmed, should weigh approximately 4 ounces. Chicken Kiev may be made with larger chicken
breasts; however, the weight suggested above is easiest to handle.

12 *tablespoons sweet butter, chilled*	2 *eggs, beaten*
3 *chicken breasts, wing bones*	⅔ *to 1 cup fine dry breadcrumbs*
attached, halved, skinned	*cooking oil or vegetable*
and boned	*shortening for deep-fat*
¾ *teaspoon salt*	*frying (about 6 cups for a*
¾ *teaspoon freshly ground pepper*	*heavy 3-quart saucepan)*
3 *tablespoons flour*	

Cut butter into 6 equal pieces (2 tablespoons each). With your hands, and the help of wax paper, shape each portion into a roll about 3 inches long and ¾ inch thick. Wrap butter portions in wax paper and freeze while preparing the chicken breasts. Cut wing tip from each breast half, leaving only the short bone that is attached to the meat to form a kind of handle. Scrape skin and meat off this bone. With a cleaver or a heavy knife, trim the joint neatly. Working carefully, cut this cleaned bone almost, but not entirely, loose from the breast half to which it is attached; bone should hang from a thread of meat and sinew and be easy to twist. Lay breast halves, smooth side down, on cutting board and trim off any fat and gristle. With a small, sharp knife and the help of your fingers, carefully pull off the small fillet attached to each breast half. Lay the breast, smooth side down, and the fillet on a sheet of wax paper and cover both with another sheet of wax paper, allowing the bone, and the part of the meat to which it is attached, to stick out. With the flat side of a cleaver, a mallet or a rolling pin, pound meat to the thickness of ⅛ inch. (Each pounded breast half will be approximately 8 inches long and 5 inches wide. Each pounded fillet will be approximately 7 inches long and 2 inches wide). Pound meat as thin as possible at the edges, since the thinner the edges, the easier it will be to seal them firmly to prevent butter from oozing out during cooking. Be careful not to tear the meat or to detach the bone from it.

To assemble the cutlets, gently peel off the wax paper from each breast half and fillet. Sprinkle evenly 1 side of each breast and fillet with ⅛ teaspoon each of salt and pepper. Place 1 portion of frozen butter in the center of each breast half. Fold the wide side of the breast half lengthwise up over butter; repeat with other side. Fold boneless end up over butter. Twist wing bone around and push bone into butter; only the ½-inch tip of the wing bone should be visible. Place fillet shawl-fashion around the bone and press it down tightly to adhere to the breast. It is essential to seal butter in tightly or it will ooze out during cooking.

Coat each cutlet on all sides with flour, shaking off excess. Dip lightly into beaten eggs, shaking off excess. Roll in breadcrumbs, coating the cutlets evenly and shaking off excess. Place cutlets in one layer on a platter and refrigerate for 1 to 2 hours. Heat the oil in a large, heavy saucepan or deep-fat fryer; the oil should reach 3 to 4 inches up the sides of the pan. Heat the oil until it registers 360°F. on a frying

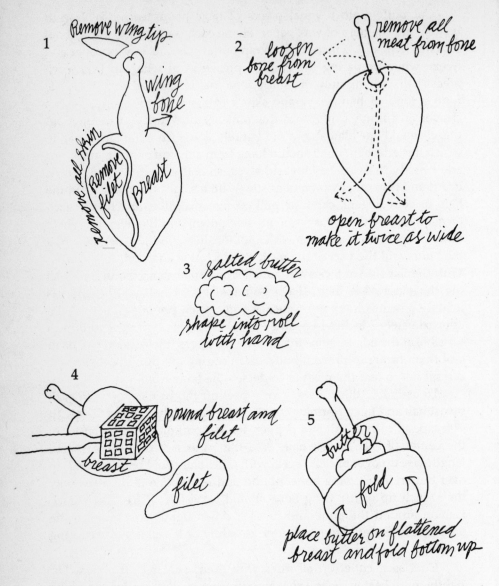

1 Remove wing tip

wing bone

remove all skin

Remove filet

Breast

2 loosen bone from breast

remove all meat from bone

open breast to make it twice as wide

3 salted butter

shape into roll with hand

4 pound breast and filet

breast

filet

5 butter

fold

place butter on flattened breast and fold bottom up

thermometer or until a 1-inch bread cube dropped into the hot oil turns golden in slightly less than 1 minute. Fry the cutlets, about 3 at a time, in the hot oil until golden brown. Cutlets should not touch each other during frying. Turn twice, using tongs or 2 spoons for turning and for removing the cutlets from the hot oil; this will prevent their being pierced. Drain on paper towels and transfer to a heated serving dish.

Keep warm in a low oven (150 to 175°F.) until all the cutlets are ready. Serve immediately, over a bed of hot cooked rice and with buttered vegetables and Mushroom Sauce (page 132).

Note: Another method is to fry the cutlets in deep fat heated to 360°F. only for 3 minutes; then place undrained cutlets in a 13- by 9-inch baking pan. Cook without a cover in a preheated moderate oven (350°F.) for about 15 minutes. Turn over twice, using tongs or two spoons. Drain on paper towels before serving.

6

roll
roll
fold

7 ← loosened bone pushed down into breast

pounded filet
rolled breast

8 Back view— pounded filet criss crosses in back

pounded filet
Rolled breast

9 flour egg bread crumbs

Roll in flour, egg, breadcrumbs
shape with hands
Roll second time in just egg and bread crumbs
shape again

Pressed Chicken Tabaká

AN UNUSUAL CHICKEN DISH FROM GEORGIA

The squab chickens are flattened, marinated and then fried until golden under a weight. Chicken Tabaká is served with Tkemali Sauce (page 81), a tart, typically Georgian prune sauce. One small chicken makes 1 serving. We introduced this dish after a trip to Georgia. It is also the specialty at our favorite restaurant in Leningrad, the Kav-Kaz (Caucasian cuisine), where the walls have brightly painted murals of Georgian life—banquets, dancing, drinking and lovemaking. We photographed the bronze door of the Kav-Kaz and had it duplicated by artists in New York as the entrance to our new Café upstairs. The scenes on the door are Georgian animal figures and part of their ancient folklore.

Serves 4

4 squab chickens or Cornish hens
    each weighing 1 to 1½
    pounds
2 cups salad oil
½ cup wine vinegar
¼ cup fresh lemon juice
2 onions, cut into wedges
2 celery ribs, sliced
1 medium carrot, sliced

1 garlic clove, chopped
1 tablespoon minced coriander
    (cilantro)
1 teaspoon dried thyme
1 teaspoon salt
½ teaspoon freshly ground pepper
6 tablespoons butter
6 tablespoons salad oil

1

cut along backbone

2

Turn over and completely remove backbone

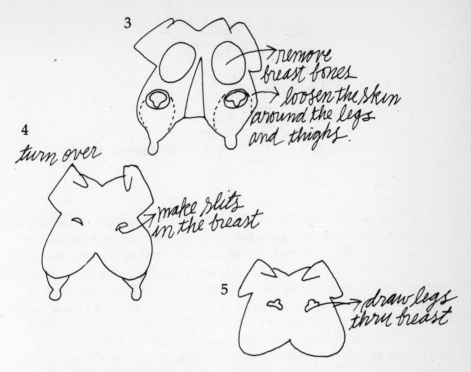

3 → remove breast bones
→ loosen the skin around the legs and thighs.

4 turn over

→ make slits in the breast

5 → draw legs thru breast

To flatten the chicken: With a sharp boning knife, cut along the length of the backbone from tail end to neck. Turn the chicken over and cut along the other side of the backbone; this frees it. Remove the backbone and lay the chicken skin side down. Press it open. Working carefully with the boning knife, cut out the breast bone and the cartilage on either side of the chicken, taking care not to tear the flesh or skin. Turn the chicken over skin side up. Twist the legs until you hear the joints crack to allow them to move freely. Cover the chicken with wax paper and pound it with a mallet or a cleaver to flatten the rib bones. Make a slit in each side of the chicken breast. Tuck the legs under the breast and pull each drumstick up through the slits in the breast; they should protrude. Bend the wing tips under the chicken. Combine the 2 cups salad oil, wine vinegar, lemon juice, onions, celery, carrot, garlic, coriander, thyme, salt and pepper in a large, rather shallow roasting pan (not aluminum). Place the flattened chickens in one layer in the marinade, making sure each is well coated with the marinade. Cover and refrigerate for 2 to 3 days, turning over frequently. Drain the chickens and pat them dry with paper towels.

6 *platter to weight birds*

saute pan

saute in butter with a weight on birds

To cook: Use 2 large (10- to 12-inch) heavy frying pans (preferably black iron skillets) to cook 2 chickens in each. Use 3 tablespoons butter and 3 tablespoons oil in each frying pan. Heat the butter and the oil. Place the flattened chickens, skin side down, in the frying pans. Put a smaller pan in each frying pan, on top of the chicken, and weigh it down as much as possible with a brick or canned foods. Over moderate to low heat, cook the chickens for about 10 minutes, or until golden brown. Remove the weighted top pans, turn the chickens with tongs and cover again with the weighted pans. Cook for another 10 minutes. Watch for any sign of burning and regulate the heat accordingly. Transfer the cooked chickens, skin side up, to a heated platter and keep warm in a low oven (150 to 175°F.). Serve hot, with Rice Pilaff (page 125) and Tkemali Sauce.

Tkemali Sauce

Makes about 2½ cups

1 *pound pitted prunes*
   water
1 *tablespoon butter*
1 *tablespoon minced onion*
1 *garlic clove, minced*
2 *tablespoons finely chopped*
   coriander (cilantro)

1½ *cups dry white wine*
¼   *teaspoon salt*
⅛   *teaspoon cayenne pepper*
1   *tablespoon fresh lemon juice*

Put the prunes in a bowl, cover with water and soak for 2 hours or until soft. Drain. Chop the prunes or process them into fine pieces in a blender or food processor. Heat the butter in a small frying pan. Add the onion and garlic and cook, stirring constantly, for 3 or 4 minutes or until soft. Add this onion mixture, the coriander, wine, salt and pepper to the prunes and return to blender or processor. Process until the consistency of sour cream. Turn into a saucepan. Cook, covered, over medium heat for 15 to 30 minutes, stirring frequently. Stir in lemon juice. Serve warm or at room temperature.

Chicken Maréchale

BAKED BONED BREAST OF CHICKEN STUFFED WITH ONIONS, MUSHROOMS AND RED WINE

Serves 6, 1 cutlet each

10 tablespoons butter
⅓ cup minced onion
½ pound mushrooms, thinly sliced
       (if large, quarter and then
       slice)
 2 tablespoons minced parsley
⅓ cup dry red wine
 1 teaspoon salt
 1 teaspoon freshly ground pepper

 6 slices firm white bread, crusts
       trimmed off
 3 chicken breasts, wing bones
       attached, halved, skinned
       and boned, each half
       weighing approximately 4
       ounces when boned
 3 tablespoons flour
 2 eggs, beaten

Heat 2 tablespoons of the butter in a large (10- to 12-inch) heavy frying pan. Add onion and cook over medium heat, stirring constantly, for 3 to 5 minutes or until soft. Add mushrooms and parsley, and cook, stirring constantly for 3 minutes more. Increase heat to medium-high. Add wine. Cook, stirring constantly, for about 5 minutes or until the wine has evaporated. Stir in ¼ teaspoon each salt and pepper; set aside. (There should be about ¾ cup (12 tablespoons) of the mixture.) Cut bread into ¼-inch cubes; there should be about 3 cups. Cut wing tip from each breast half, leaving only the short bone attached to the meat to form a handle. Scrape skin and meat off this bone and, with a cleaver or heavy knife, trim the joint neatly. Working carefully, cut this cleaned bone almost, but not entirely, loose from the breast half to which it is attached; bone should hang from a thread of meat and sinew and be easy to twist. Lay breast halves, smooth side down, on a cutting board and trim off any fat and gristle. With a small, sharp knife and the help of your fingers, carefully pull off the small fillet attached to each breast half. Lay breast, smooth side down, and fillet on a sheet of wax paper and cover with another sheet of wax paper, letting the bone and the part of the meat to which it is attached stick out. With the flat side of a cleaver, a mallet or a rolling pin, pound meat to the thickness of ⅛ inch. (Each pounded breast half will be approximately 8 inches long and 5 inches wide. Each pounded fillet will be approximately 7 inches long and 2 inches wide.) Pound meat as thinly as possible at the edges, since the thinner the edges, the easier it will be to seal them firmly to prevent the filling from oozing out during cooking. Be careful not to tear the meat nor to detach the bone from it.

To assemble the cutlets, gently peel off wax paper from breast halves and fillets. Sprinkle evenly one side of each breast half and fillet with salt and pepper. Place about 2 tablespoons mushroom filling in the center of each breast half and cover with fillet, seasoned side down. Fold the wide side of the breast half lengthwise up over filling; repeat with other side. Fold boneless end over filling. Twist wing bone around and push in only enough to enclose and seal in the filling; bone should stick out like a short handle. It is essential to seal in the filling tightly or it will ooze out during cooking. Coat each cutlet on all sides with flour, shaking off excess. Dip lightly into beaten eggs, shaking off excess. Press into bread cubes until all sides are coated and cubes are sticking to the meat. Place cutlets in one layer on a platter and refrigerate for 1 to 2 hours.

To cook, heat 4 tablespoons of the remaining butter in a large (10-inch) heavy frying pan. Add 3 cutlets and cook over medium heat for 5 to 7 minutes or until golden brown on all sides. Turn several times with tongs or two spoons to prevent piercing the cutlets. Place browned cutlets into a 13- by 9-inch baking pan and keep warm in a low oven (150 to 175°F.). Reduce heat to low and add remaining 4 tablespoons butter. Add remaining 3 cutlets to the frying pan and cook for 5 to 7 minutes or until golden brown on all sides, turning several times with tongs or two spoons. Place cutlets in baking pan with the first batch, keeping all in one layer. Turn oven heat to medium (350°F.). Cook cutlets without a cover for 20 to 25 minutes, or until thoroughly cooked through, turning twice with tongs or two spoons. Serve immediately over a bed of hot cooked rice, with a vegetable and Chicken Velouté Sauce (page 134).

Note: This recipe can also be successfully made with chicken breasts that are halved, skinned and boned as above, but without wing bones.

⚜ ⚜ ⚜ ⚜ ⚜ ⚜ ⚜

Cotelette de Volaille

CHICKEN BREASTS STUFFED WITH A SAVORY GROUND CHICKEN FILLING AND BAKED TO A GOLDEN BROWN

It is said that the great Chaliapin favored this specialty the most.

Serves 6, 1 cutlet each

6 *chicken drumsticks (approximately 1½ pounds), skinned, boned, gristle removed and ground, or about 1¼ cup (10 ounces) firmly packed ground, uncooked chicken*

6 *tablespoons sweet butter, at room temperature*

6 *to 8 slices firm white bread, crusts trimmed off*

3 *chicken breasts, wing bones attached, halved, skinned and boned, each breast half weighing approximately 4 ounces when boned*

1 *teaspoon salt*

¼ *teaspoon freshly ground pepper*

3 *tablespoons flour*

2 *eggs, beaten*

8 *tablespoons butter*

Mix together the ground chicken meat and the sweet butter. Blend thoroughly into a smooth, even mixture. Using about ¼ cup of the mixture for each portion, divide it into 6 equal portions. Shape each portion into oval patties, each measuring 3 by 1 by ½ inches. If necessary, moisten hands with cold water to facilitate shaping. Chill 1 to 2 hours, or until very firm. Cut bread into ¼-inch cubes and reserve. (There should be 3 to 4 cups bread cubes.) Cut wing tip from each breast half, leaving only the short bone attached to the meat, forming a kind of handle. Scrape skin and meat off this bone and with a cleaver or heavy knife, trim the joint neatly. Working carefully, cut this bone almost, but not entirely, loose from the breast half to which it is attached; bone should hang from a twist of meat and sinew and be easy to twist. Lay breast halves, smooth side down, on a cutting board and trim off any fat and gristle. With a small, sharp knife and the help of your fingers, carefully pull off the small fillet attached to each breast half. Lay breast, smooth side down, and the fillet on a sheet of wax paper and cover with another sheet of wax paper, letting the bone and the part of the meat to which it is attached stick out. With the flat side of a cleaver, a mallet or a rolling pin, pound meat ⅛ inch thick. (Each pounded breast half will be approximately 8 inches long and 5 inches wide. Each pounded fillet will be approximately 7 inches long and 2 inches wide.) Pound meat as thinly as possible at the edges, since the thinner the edges, the easier it will be to seal them firmly to prevent the filling from oozing out while cooking. Be careful not to tear the meat or to detach the bone from it. To assemble the cutlets, gently peel off wax paper from breast halves and fillets. Sprinkle evenly one side of each breast half and each fillet with the salt and pepper. Place 1 oval patty of filling in the center of each breast half and cover with fillet, seasoned side down. Fold the wide side of the breast half lengthwise up over filling; repeat with the other side. Fold boneless end over filling. Twist wing bone around and push into filling; only about ½ inch of the wing bone tip should be visible. It is essential to seal in the filling tightly or it will ooze out during cooking.

Coat each cutlet on all sides with flour, shaking off excess. Dip lightly into beaten eggs, shaking off excess. Press into bread cubes until all sides are coated and cubes are sticking to the meat. Place cutlets in one layer on a platter and chill 1 to 2 hours.

To cook, heat 4 tablespoons of the butter in a large (10- to 12-inch), heavy frying pan. Add 3 cutlets and cook over medium heat for 5 to 7 minutes or until golden brown on all sides. Turn several times with tongs or two spoons to prevent piercing the cutlets. Place browned cutlets into a 13- by 9-inch baking pan and keep warm in a low oven (150 to 175°F.). Reduce heat to low and add the remaining 4 tablespoons butter to the frying pan. Add remaining 3 cutlets and cook for 5 to 7 minutes or until golden brown on all sides, turning several times with tongs or two spoons. Place cutlets in baking pan with the first batch, keeping all in one layer. Turn oven heat to medium (350°F.). Cook cutlets without a cover for about 35 minutes or until, when a knife is inserted in the middle of a cutlet, the inside no longer shows pink and is thoroughly cooked. Serve immediately on a bed of hot cooked rice, with vegetables and Madeira Sauce (page 132).

Note: The recipe can also be successfully made with chicken breasts that are halved, skinned and boned as above, but without wing bones.

Chicken Chakhobili

SPRING CHICKEN STEWED WITH TOMATOES AND ONIONS EN CASSEROLE

Chakhobili has a lovely Georgian touch—the southern, Mediterranean influence on Russian cuisine. It is a Peter Martins favorite.

Serves 6

SAUCE

3 tablespoons cooking oil	½ cup dry white wine
2 medium onions, minced	1 teaspoon salt
1 large garlic clove, minced	½ teaspoon freshly ground pepper
1 can (1 pound 12 ounces) Italian-style tomatoes, undrained—about 3½ cups	½ teaspoon ground coriander, or 2 tablespoons fresh chopped coriander leaves, or ½ teaspoon dried thyme
1 can (6 ounces) tomato paste	

---

2 2½-pound chickens, cut into serving pieces	2 tablespoons butter
1 tablespoon cooking oil	2 tablespoons lemon juice

First, make the sauce. In a heavy 4-quart saucepan or Dutch oven, heat the oil. Add onions and garlic and cook over medium heat, stirring constantly, for 5 to 8 minutes, or until soft and golden; do not brown. Add canned tomatoes and tomato paste and mix well. Stir in wine, salt, pepper, coriander or thyme. Bring to boiling point and turn heat to low. Simmer, covered, for about 20 minutes, stirring frequently.

While sauce is cooking, trim all excess fat from chicken pieces. Cut off wing tips and backbone pieces and save or freeze for another use. Heat the oil and the butter in a large, heavy frying pan. Add a few chicken pieces and brown over medium heat on all sides. Transfer browned chicken pieces to sauce as done and brown remaining pieces. When all the chicken pieces have been added to the sauce, cover the pot and cook over low to medium heat, stirring frequently, for about 30 minutes or until chicken pieces are tender. If sauce is too thin, cook without a cover until it reaches desired consistency. Skim off fat. Remove from heat, check the seasoning and stir in the lemon juice. Serve in a heated deep serving dish over a bed of hot cooked rice.

Bitochki

CHOPPED CHICKEN AND VEAL PATTIES, SERVED WITH SAUCE STROGANOFF

One of the much-loved cotelette family of Russian cuisine.

Serves 6, 2 patties each

4 tablespoons butter
1 medium onion, minced
½ cup minced parsley
2 pounds uncooked boned and
   skinned chicken breasts,
   ground (see below)
1 pound lean veal, ground (see
   below)

½ cup heavy cream
1 egg
1 teaspoon salt
½ teaspoon freshly ground pepper
⅔ cup fine dry breadcrumbs

Heat 1 tablespoon of the butter in a heavy frying pan. Add onion and parsley and cook over medium heat, stirring constantly, for 3 to 5 minutes or until soft; do not brown. In a large bowl combine chicken, veal, onion mixture, heavy cream, egg, salt and pepper. Using a round ½-cup measure, divide mixture into 12 equal portions. Shape each portion into 3- or 4-inch round patties, ½ to ¾ inches thick. Roll patties in breadcrumbs, coating them evenly and lightly and shaking off excess crumbs. Heat 1 tablespoon of the remaining butter in a large (10-inch) heavy frying pan. Add 4 patties in one layer. Cook over medium heat for 10 to 12 minutes, turning over once; patties should be golden brown. With a wide spatula, transfer patties to a heated serving dish and keep hot in a low oven (150° to 175°F.). Repeat twice with remaining butter and patties, adding patties to serving dish as they are done. Serve with Sauce Stroganoff (page 129).

Note: To prepare 2 pounds uncooked boned and skinned chicken breast for grinding: remove bones, skin and fat from 4 pounds chicken breasts, or remove skin and fat from 8 boneless chicken cutlets weighing approximately 2 pounds. Use food processor for grinding or push through meat grinder once.

To prepare 1 pound lean veal for grinding, use boneless veal shoulder. Since all fat and gristle must be trimmed off the meat, you will need 1½ pounds boneless veal to get 1 pound lean veal for grinding. Use food processor for grinding or push through meat grinder once.

Cotelettes Boyar

CHOPPED VEAL AND CHICKEN PATTIES

These are named after the Boyars, the officials who served the czars in early days and gained princely powers and vast fortunes, thus becoming the only Russian nobility at that time.

Serves 6, 3 patties each

5 *tablespoons butter*
1 *medium onion, minced*
½ *cup minced parsley*
2 *pounds lean veal, ground (see below)*
1 *pound uncooked boned and skinned chicken breasts, ground (see below)*

⅓ *cup heavy cream*
1 *egg*
1 *teaspoon salt*
½ *teaspoon freshly ground pepper*
fine dry breadcrumbs

Heat 1 tablespoon of the butter in a heavy frying pan. Add onion and parsley and cook over medium heat, stirring constantly, for 3 to 5 minutes or until soft; do not brown. In a large bowl combine ground veal, chicken, onion mixture, cream, egg, salt and pepper. Mix very thoroughly. Using a rounded ⅓-cup measure for each portion, divide meat mixture into 18 equal portions. Shape each portion into oval patties, each measuring 4 by 2 by 1½ inches. Roll patties in breadcrumbs, coating them evenly and lightly and shaking off excess crumbs. Heat 2 tablespoons of the butter in a large (10 or 12-inch) heavy frying pan. Add half the patties in one layer. Cook over medium heat about 12 to 15 minutes, or until golden brown, turning twice to ensure even browning. With a wide spatula, transfer cooked patties to a heated serving dish and keep warm in a low oven (150° to 175°F.). Repeat with the remaining butter and patties. Serve with Sauce Espagnole (page 130), with hot, cooked rice.

Note: To prepare 2 pounds of lean veal for grinding, you will need 3 pounds of boneless veal shoulder, since all fat and gristle must first be trimmed off the meat. Use food processor for grinding or push through meat grinder once.

To prepare 1 pound uncooked boned and skinned chicken breasts for grinding, remove bones, skins and fat from 2 pounds chicken breasts; or remove skin and fat from 4 boneless chicken cutlets weighing approximately 1 pound. Use food processor for grinding or push through meat grinder once.

Cotelettes Pojarski

CHOPPED BEEF AND VEAL PATTIES SERVED WITH MUSHROOM SAUCE

This dish is named after an innkeeper in Torjok, between Moscow and St. Petersburg, where in the old days people traveling by carriage used to change horses. Pojarski originally made the cotelettes from ground venison and other ground meats or fish.

Serves 6, 2 cotelettes each

5   tablespoons butter
1   medium onion, minced
½   cup minced parsley
1½ pounds lean veal, ground (see below)
1½ pounds ground beef
½   cup heavy cream
1   teaspoon salt
¼   teaspoon freshly ground pepper
1   teaspoon prepared mustard, preferably Dijon
¼   teaspoon ground coriander
⅛   teaspoon Tabasco
⅔   cup fine dry breadcrumbs
3   tablespoons cooking oil

Heat 2 tablespoons of the butter in a heavy frying pan. Add onion and parsley and cook over medium heat, stirring constantly, for 3 to 5 minutes or until soft; do not brown. In a large bowl combine ground veal, beef, onion mixture, heavy cream, salt, pepper, mustard, coriander and Tabasco. Mix thoroughly. Using a rounded ½-cup measure for each portion, divide meat mixture into 12 equal portions. Shape each portion into oval patties, each measuring 5 by 3 by ¾ inches. Roll patties in breadcrumbs, coating them evenly and lightly, shaking off excess crumbs. Heat 1 tablespoon of the remaining butter and 1 tablespoon cooking oil in a large (10-inch) heavy frying pan. Add 4 patties and cook over medium heat about 3 minutes, turning once and cooking 3 more minutes; patties should be golden brown. With a wide spatula, transfer patties to a 15- by 10- by 1-inch jelly-roll or baking pan. Repeat twice with remaining patties, butter and cooking oil. Bake in a preheated moderate (350°F.) oven for about 15 minutes or until patties are cooked through. To check, cut into center of one patty—meat should be golden brown throughout, with no trace of pink. Patties can also be cooked over direct heat for the entire time—12 to 15 minutes, turning once. Serve with Mushroom Sauce (page 132).

Note: To prepare 1 pound lean veal for grinding you will need 1½ pounds of boneless veal shoulder, since all fat and gristle must be trimmed off. Use food processor or push through meat grinder once.

Chicken Pojarski

GROUND CHICKEN PATTIES SAUTEED IN BUTTER

Serves 6, 3 patties each

16 *slices firm white bread, without crusts*
1   *cup milk*
3   *pounds ground uncooked chicken breasts (see below)*
½   *cup minced mushrooms (approximately 2 ounces)*
¼   *cup minced parsley*
1   *teaspoon salt*
¼   *teaspoon freshly ground pepper*
4   *egg yolks*
3   *tablespoons flour*
6   *tablespoons butter*
6   *tablespoons cooking oil*

Soak 4 slices of the bread in the milk for about 5 minutes or until thoroughly saturated. Squeeze out the bread with your hands. Cut the remaining bread into ¼-inch cubes; there will be about 6 cups of bread cubes. In a large bowl, combine the soaked bread, the chicken, mushrooms, parsley, salt, pepper and 1 egg yolk. Mix thoroughly with a wooden spoon. Using a rounded ⅓-cup measure for each portion, divide mixture into 18 equal portions. Shape each portion into 3-inch patties with your moistened hands. Beat remaining egg yolks slightly. Coat both sides of the patties lightly with flour and shake off excess flour. Brush both sides of the patties with egg yolk; then press into bread cubes until both sides of the patties are coated. Heat 2 tablespoons butter and 2 tablespoons oil in a large (10-inch), heavy frying pan. Add 6 patties. Cook over medium heat, turning once, for 3 to 4 minutes or until browned. Lower heat and cook, turning twice, for 6 to 8 more minutes, or until no longer pink in the center; check by piercing a patty with the point of a sharp knife. Be careful not to scorch patties. Remove with a slotted spoon to a heated serving dish and keep warm in a low oven (150 to 175°F.). Repeat twice with remaining butter, oil and patties. Serve with kasha, a buttered vegetable and Sherried Sauce Bechamel (page 133).

Note: To prepare 3 pounds uncooked chicken breasts for grinding, remove bones, skin and fat from 6 pounds chicken breasts; or remove skin and fat from 12 boneless chicken cutlets weighing approximately 3 pounds.

Zrazy à la Nelson

BEEF ROLLS STUFFED WITH A SAVORY MUSHROOM FILLING

Serves 6, 1 roll each

6 slices lean top round or beef
    rump, ¼ inch thick and
    measuring 10 to 12 inches
    by 4 to 6 inches (total
    weight approximately 1½
    pounds)
  salt
  freshly ground pepper
3 tablespoons butter

1 medium onion, minced
¼ pound mushrooms, trimmed and
    finely chopped
¾ cup fresh white breadcrumbs
2 tablespoons minced parsley
1 egg yolk
1 cup beef bouillon
2 tablespoons tomato paste

Trim all fat and gristle from the meat. Place each slice of meat between 2 sheets of wax paper. With a mallet or a rolling pin, pound slices to ⅛-inch thickness. Be careful not to tear the meat. Sprinkle both sides of each slice of meat with salt and pepper; you will need a total of approximately ¾ teaspoon salt and ½ teaspoon pepper. Heat 2 tablespoons of the butter in a large (10-inch), heavy frying pan. Add onion. Cook over medium heat, stirring constantly, for 3 to 5 minutes, or until soft and golden. Add mushrooms. Cook, stirring all the time, for about 2 minutes. Remove from heat. Stir in breadcrumbs, parsley, egg yolk, ⅓ teaspoon salt and ⅛ teaspoon pepper. Mix thoroughly. Place about 2 tablespoons onion mixture on the narrow side of each slice of meat. Roll up jelly-roll fashion. Secure with kitchen thread. Heat remaining tablespoon butter in a large (10-inch), heavy frying pan. Add beef rolls and cook over medium heat for 5 to 7 minutes turning over frequently, until browned on all sides. Transfer meat rolls in one layer to a 10- by 6-inch baking pan or to an 8-inch-square baking pan. Combine bouillon and tomato paste and pour over the rolls. Cover pan with aluminum foil. Cook in a preheated low oven (325°F.) for 1 to 1½ hours or until tender when pierced with a fork. Turn rolls 3 times during the cooking. Transfer meat rolls to a heated serving dish and remove kitchen thread. Spoon pan juices over rolls; there will be approximately 1⅓ cups. Serve with mashed potatoes or over a bed of hot cooked rice, with pan gravy.

Note: Double the recipe for very hungry people.

Roast Leg of Lamb à la Russe

Serves 8 to 10

1 *leg of lamb, weighing 6½ to 7*
  pounds with bone in (boned
  meat will weigh
  approximately 5½ pounds)
1 *teaspoon salt*
¼ *teaspoon freshly ground pepper*
  grated rind of 1 lemon

juice of 2 large lemons
1 *large onion, sliced*
2 *large carrots, chopped*
2 *celery ribs, without leaves,*
  chopped
2 *cups beef bouillon*
½ *to 1 cup dry white wine*

Preheat oven to low (325°F.). Have butcher bone the lamb or do it yourself. Peel fell from lamb and trim off any fat. Spread lamb out flat on wax paper on kitchen counter. Sprinkle with salt, pepper and lemon rind. Sprinkle with the lemon juice and with your hands, massage juice into meat. Roll meat up jelly-roll style and tie at 2-inch intervals. Combine onion, carrots and celery and spread over the bottom of a large, shallow roasting pan. Place rolled lamb on vegetables. Pour bouillon over meat and vegetables. Roast, uncovered, for 2 to 2½ or 2¾ hours, depending on degree of doneness desired. Baste frequently with pan juices. Transfer lamb to a heated platter and keep warm in a low oven (150 to 175°F.). Bring pan juices and vegetables to the boiling point and skim off all grease. Puree in a blender or food processor, or push through a sieve. Return to pan and add ½ to 1 cup white wine depending on consistency of the gravy you prefer. Bring quickly to the boiling point, stirring constantly, and cook for 1 minute. Carve lamb and place on a heated deep platter. Spoon a little of the gravy over the meat and pass the rest in a sauceboat—or if there is little gravy, spoon it all over the meat. Serve with Boiled Potatoes (page 124), buttered vegetables and Sauce Madeira (page 132).

Luli Kebab à la Russian Tea Room

Luli Kebab differs enough from its counterpart, chopped sirloin, to delight the taste buds. We serve it with our Russian mustard, which is really hot! Eggplant Orientale is a lovely accompaniment.

Serves 6, 2 patties each

3 tablespoons butter	2 teaspoons salt
¾ cup minced onion (1 medium-to-large onion)	¾ teaspoon freshly ground pepper
3 pounds ground leg of lamb	3 eggs, lightly beaten
	¾ teaspoon ground coriander

Heat the butter in a large saucepan. Add the onion and cook over medium heat, for 3 to 5 minutes or until soft. Remove from heat and add meat, salt, pepper, eggs and coriander. Mix very thoroughly with a wooden spoon. Using a rounded ½-cup measure for each portion, divide meat mixture into 12 equal portions. Shape each portion into a sausage-shaped patty measuring about 5 by 3 inches. Place patties on an oiled broiler grid. Broil 4 inches from the source of heat for 10 to 15 minutes, turning patties frequently with tongs or two spoons. Patties should be golden brown and cooked through. Serve on a bed of hot cooked rice, with sautéed red and green peppers, Brown Sauce (page 130) and mustard (see Russian Tea Room Mustard, below).

The Russian Tea Room Mustard

Makes about ⅓ cup

4 tablespoons dry mustard	2 teaspoons hot water
1 tablespoon brown sugar	1 teaspoon sesame oil
2 teaspoons vinegar	

Combine ingredients in a bowl and blend thoroughly. Chill before using with Pelmeny and other dishes.

Tefteli (Sour Clops)

POACHED MEATBALLS IN LEMON AND CAPER SAUCE

Serves 6, 3 meatballs each

MEATBALLS

3 *slices white bread without crusts*
¾ *cup milk*
2 *tablespoons butter*
1 *small onion, minced*
1 *pound ground round, ground twice*
1 *pound lean boneless veal, ground twice*

2 *flat anchovy fillets, drained and mashed, or 2 teaspoons anchovy paste*
   grated rind of ½ small lemon
2 *eggs, lightly beaten*
½ *teaspoon salt*
¼ *teaspoon freshly ground pepper*

Soak the bread in the milk for 5 minutes or until it is thoroughly saturated. With your hands, squeeze the bread dry and reserve. Heat the butter in a small frying pan. Add onion. Cook over medium heat, stirring constantly, for 3 to 5 minutes or until soft. Turn all the meat into a large bowl. Add the bread, onion, anchovy fillets or paste, grated lemon rind, eggs, salt and pepper. Knead vigorously with both hands until all the ingredients are thoroughly blended. (Moisten your hands occasionally with cold water to prevent sticking). Using a rounded ¼-cup measure, divide the mixture into 18 portions. With moistened hands, shape each portion into a ball. Place on a platter and refrigerate until cooking time.

POACHING LIQUID

2 *quarts beef bouillon (made with bouillon cubes if desired)*
1 *medium onion, peeled, stuck with 4 cloves*

2 *bay leaves*

Combine all ingredients in a large heavy saucepan or soup kettle. Bring to the boiling point. Cook over medium heat, uncovered, for 10 minutes. Reduce heat to low. Carefully drop the meatballs into the poaching liquid. Simmer, uncovered, for 20 to 25 minutes. Transfer meatballs with a slotted spoon to a deep, heated serving dish. Cover with aluminum foil—meatballs darken when exposed to air. Keep warm in a low oven (150 to 175°F.). Strain the poaching liquid into a bowl and reserve.

SAUCE

6 *tablespoons butter*	2 *tablespoons drained capers*
6 *tablespoons flour*	2 *egg yolks, beaten*
2 *cups poaching liquid*	2 *to 3 tablespoons sour cream*
1 *cup dry white wine*	⅓ *teaspoon sugar*
1 *tablespoon fresh lemon juice*	

Heat the butter in a large, heavy frying pan. Stir in the flour. Cook over low to medium heat, stirring constantly, for 1 or 2 minutes; the mixture must remain pale. Stir in the poaching liquid and the wine. Cook, stirring constantly with a wire whisk or a wooden spoon, until the sauce thickens and is smooth. Reduce heat to low. Stir in the lemon juice and the capers. Cook, uncovered, stirring frequently, for about 10 minutes. Stir about ¼ cup of the sauce into the egg yolks and blend thoroughly. Return mixture to sauce and mix well. Stir in the sour cream. Check the seasoning; if necessary, add a little salt and pepper. Add the sugar; the sauce should have a touch of sweetness. Return meatballs to sauce. Simmer, uncovered, until they are heated through, basting them frequently with the sauce. Do not boil or the sauce will curdle. To serve, turn meatballs and sauce into a heated serving dish. Serve with kasha and a green vegetable.

Ham à la Russe

The Russian Tea Room often serves Ham à la Russe for Russian Easter dinner. Tradition says that birds were not served in Russia at Easter because they were let free to fly, bringing the news that Christ had risen.

Serves 6

2 *pounds lean cooked ham, ¼ inch thick*
2 *tablespoons butter*
1 *tablespoon cooking oil*
2 *teaspoons flour*

½ *cup Madeira*
3 *tablespoons water*
¾ *cup sour cream*
⅛ *to ¼ teaspoon freshly ground pepper*

Trim fat from ham. Make small incisions around edges to prevent curling during cooking. Cut ham into serving pieces; the number depends on the shape of the ham slices (round or rectangular) but there should be 3 to 4 pieces for each serving. Blot ham slices dry on both sides with paper towels. Heat butter and oil in a large (10-inch) heavy frying pan. Add as many ham slices as frying pan will hold in 1 layer and without touching. Cook ham over medium heat for about 1 minute on each side or until lightly browned. Transfer cooked ham to heated serving dish and keep hot in a low oven (150 to 175°F.). Repeat with remaining ham and, if necessary, lower the heat. Remove rest of ham to the serving dish. If there is too much fat left from frying ham, pour off all but 1 teaspoon. Reduce heat to low. Stir flour into pan drippings. Cook for 1 minute. Stir in Madeira and water. Cook, stirring constantly, until sauce is smooth and thickened. Stir in sour cream, pepper and any juices in the serving dish containing the cooked ham. Cook, stirring all the time, until sauce is heated through, but do not boil. Spoon sauce over ham, allowing about 2½ tablespoons for each serving, or serve sauce separately.

Note: For double the amount of sauce, use 2 teaspoons fat, 4 teaspoons flour, 1 cup Madeira, ⅓ cup water, 1¼ to 1½ cups sour cream, and pepper to taste. Proceed as above.

Veal Soblianka

A DELICATE COMBINATION OF VEAL AND MUSHROOMS

Serves 6

1 *pound mushrooms*
4 *tablespoons butter*
1 *tablespoon flour*
6 *boneless veal cutlets,*
   approximately 7 by 4
   inches, ¼ inch thick (about
   1½ pounds)

1½ *teaspoons salt*
¾ *teaspoon freshly ground pepper,*
   preferably white
⅓ *cup sour cream*

Turn the mushrooms into a bowl filled with cold water and wash them quickly, swishing them around with your hands. Drain and dry thoroughly between several thicknesses of paper towels. Cut the mushrooms into thin slices. Heat 2 tablespoons of the butter in a large (10- or 12-inch), heavy frying pan. Cook over medium heat, stirring constantly, for about 5 minutes, or until mushrooms are tender but still retain their light color and their shape. Stir in flour and cook for 1 more minute. Transfer mushrooms to a bowl and reserve.

Dry the cutlets between paper towels and sprinkle each cutlet on both sides with a little salt and pepper. Heat the remaining butter in the frying pan in which the mushrooms have been cooked. Add the cutlets and cook for 4 or 5 minutes on one side. Turn and cook for 3 more minutes, or until cooked through. Test by inserting the point of a sharp knife into a cutlet; if the juices run yellow rather than pink, the meat is done. Stir sour cream into the mushrooms. Add salt and pepper to taste. Pile the mushrooms on top of the cutlets in the frying pan. Turn heat to low and cover the pan. Heat gently until mushrooms are warmed through, but do not boil. Using a broad spatula, transfer to a heated serving dish and serve immediately, with mashed potatoes, buttered spinach and Horseradish Sauce (page 135).

Kulebiaka

A SALMON OR CABBAGE LOAF (OR CHICKEN OR TURKEY) BAKED IN A PASTRY SHELL WITH RICE, EGGS AND MUSHROOMS, SERVED WITH A CREAM SAUCE

This dish is the Russian Beef Wellington and well worth the effort it takes to prepare, as it makes a beautiful presentation. It keeps hot because it's sliced at the table. It can be prepared ahead for weekend company, and needs only a green salad as accompaniment. Its versatility is appealing, too—any filling—meat, chicken, cabbage or fish—will work very well.

Serves 6 to 12

PASTRY

4 *cups sifted flour*
1 *teaspoon salt*
½ *pound butter, chilled*

⅓ *cup solid shortening, chilled*
8 *to 10 tablespoons ice water*

Combine flour and salt in a large bowl. Using a pastry blender or 2 knives, cut in butter and shortening until mixture resembles coarse crumbs. Gradually add 8 tablespoons of ice water, mixing lightly and quickly with a fork until the texture sticks together and forms into a ball. If the dough seems crumbly, add up to 2 more tablespoons ice water, ¼ teaspoon at a time. Wrap dough in wax paper and chill 3 hours or longer. (If the dough is chilled longer, it will need time to stand at room temperature to become sufficiently pliable to roll out.)

CREPES

½ *cup unsifted flour*
¼ *teaspoon salt*
2 *eggs*

⅓ *cup milk*
1 *tablespoon butter, melted*

Combine flour and salt in a small bowl. In another small bowl, combine eggs, milk and melted butter; mix lightly. Add to the flour mixture. Using a rotary beater, a wire whisk or an electric beater at low speed, beat mixture until well blended and smooth. There should be a little over 1 cup of batter. Slowly heat a 6- or 7-inch crepe or frying pan until a drop of water evaporates immediately when dropped on the surface. Have ready a small container of melted butter and a brush. Brush pan very lightly with melted butter. Pour batter, 2 tablespoons at a time, into heated pan and quickly rotate the pan to spread the batter evenly. Cook over medium heat until bottom is slightly browned and the top is set; turn and lightly brown the other side. Remove to a plate. Repeat with remaining batter; if needed, butter the pan lightly between crepes. When cool, stack crepes with wax paper between each until ready to use. Yield: 8 crepes.

SALMON FILLING

¾ *cup water*
¾ *cup dry white wine*
2 *teaspoons salt*
1 *onion slice*
1 *lemon slice*
1½ *pounds fresh salmon, cut into*
    steaks
3 *tablespoons butter*
1 *large onion, minced*

½ *pound mushrooms, thinly sliced*
2 *tablespoons lemon juice*
3 *cups cooked rice (1 cup*
    uncooked)
5 *hard-cooked eggs, peeled and*
    coarsely chopped
¼ *cup minced fresh dill weed*
2 *tablespoons minced parsley*
¼ *teaspoon freshly ground pepper*

In a large, deep frying pan or saucepan combine the water, wine, 1 teaspoon of the salt and the onion and lemon slices. Bring to the boiling point and add salmon. Reduce heat to low. Cook, covered, for about 15 minutes or just until fish flakes easily with a fork. Drain. Remove skin and bones from the salmon and discard. Flake salmon. There will be about 1 pound of salmon, or approximately 2⅔ cups. Heat the butter in a large (10- to 12-inch) heavy frying pan. Add the minced onion. Cook over medium heat, stirring constantly, for about 3 to 5 minutes, or until soft; do not brown. Add mushrooms. Cook, stirring all the time, for about 3 minutes or until barely tender. Remove from heat, add lemon juice and toss mixture. In a large bowl combine flaked salmon, onion, rice, chopped eggs, dill, parsley, the remaining teaspoon of salt and pepper. Mix quickly and gently with a fork to blend together—but no more. There will be approximately 8 cups of the salmon-rice mixture. Refrigerate until ready to use.

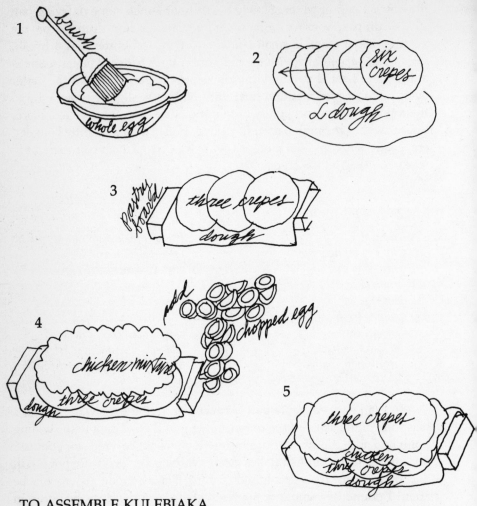

TO ASSEMBLE KULEBIAKA

Lightly butter a baking sheet measuring at least 14 by 17 inches. Preheat oven to hot (400°F.). If necessary, bring chilled dough back to room temperature for rolling out. Snip off a small 2-inch ball of dough and reserve it for later decoration. On a floured surface, and using, preferably, a floured pastry cloth and a stockinette-covered rolling pin, roll dough into a 14- by 16-inch rectangle. Carefully fold the 14-inch side of the dough over in half (that is, dough is folded horizontally). Transfer dough to the baking sheet, placing it in the middle of the baking sheet's long side. Unfold dough back to a rectangle. Lightly beat

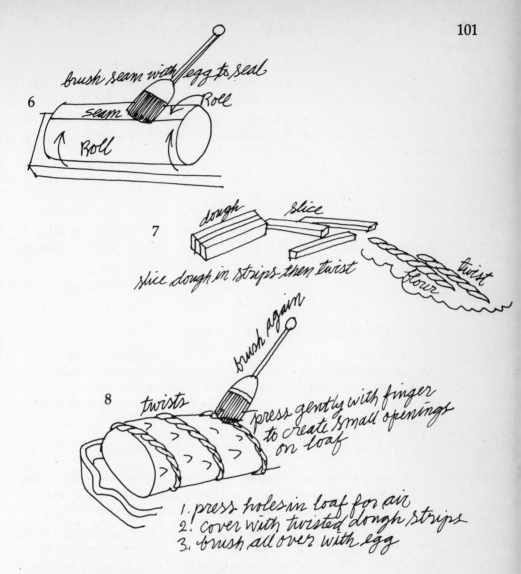

6 brush seam with egg to seal · seam · Roll · Roll

7 dough · slice · slice dough in strips then twist · flour · twist

8 twists · brush again · press gently with finger to create small openings on loaf
1. press holes in loaf for air
2. cover with twisted dough strips
3. brush all over with egg

1 egg and lightly brush the whole surface of the dough rectangle with beaten egg. Place 4 crepes, overlapping each other, in the middle of the dough, leaving about 4 inches of dough on either side. Spoon salmon mixture over crepes. Top with remaining crepes. Bring one side of the dough up over crepes and filling. Repeat with other side. Tuck in open ends. Press edges and ends together firmly to seal in the filling. The shaped dough should form a rectangle measuring approximately 5 by 15 inches. Turn the loaf over, seam side down. Make 2 or 3 V-shaped slits at each end of the loaf to allow steam to escape during baking. Roll

out the reserved 2-inch ball of dough to approximately ¼-inch thickness. Cut dough into ½-inch strips or any desired shape (diamonds, clover leaves, etc.) for decoration. Place on center of loaf. Brush loaf and decorations with remaining beaten egg. Bake for about 1 hour, or until golden brown. Serve immediately with Fish Velouté Sauce (page 134).

CHICKEN FILLING FOR KULEBIAKA

Proceed as for Salmon Filling but substitute for the salmon 2½ to 3 cups cooked chicken cut into ¼-inch dice. Serve with Sauce Bechamel (page 133).

CABBAGE FILLING FOR KULEBIAKA

4 quarts water
18 cups shredded cabbage
    (approximately 3 pounds)
4 tablespoons butter
2 large onions, minced
4 hard-cooked eggs, coarsely
    chopped
¼ cup minced fresh dill weed
2 tablespoons minced parsley
2 teaspoons salt
¼ teaspoon freshly ground pepper
½ teaspoon sugar

Pour the water into a large soup kettle or saucepan and bring to the boiling point. Add cabbage and bring again to the boiling point. Reduce heat to medium and cook, uncovered, for 5 minutes. Drain and set aside. There will be approximately 6 cups of cooked cabbage. Heat butter in a large saucepan. Add onions and cook over medium heat, stirring constantly, for about 5 minutes or until soft; do not brown. Add drained cabbage. Turn heat to low. Cook, covered, for about 30 minutes, or until soft, stirring frequently. The cabbage should be completely dry. If not, remove the cover and cook over high heat, stirring constantly, until dry. Remove from heat and stir in eggs, dill, parsley, salt, pepper and sugar. There will be approximately 7 cups of filling. Cool before filling the Kulebiaka.

Serve with Bechamel Sauce (page 133) but add 1 tablespoon tomato paste to the sauce just before it begins to boil.

Note: One 4-pound cabbage, core and outer leaves removed, will yield approximately 3 pounds, or 18 cups, of shredded raw cabbage.

Pelmeny Siberian

MEAT-FILLED LITTLE DUMPLINGS, SIMILAR TO ITALIAN RAVIOLI AND TORTELLINI

The origin of pelmeny is Siberian, and since they freeze well, Siberian housewives used to make them in large quantities and keep them in the snow outside the kitchen window. When the time came to cook them, which was often, the pelmeny were plunged into boiling broth. Pelmeny with uncooked filling should be small or the filling won't cook through. They are served in a clear bouillon, with a mustard sauce, and sour cream on the side, with plenty of fresh dill. If pelmeny are to be served as a main dish, double this recipe. You may also make several batches at one time and freeze them.

At The Russian Tea Room they are the piece de résistance at Wednesday lunch only, a tradition that goes back at least 30 years. Pelmeny are a favorite of Mrs. Jacqueline Onassis and director Mike Nichols.

Serves 6, 10 Pelmeny each

DOUGH

2 cups unsifted flour
1 teaspoon salt

1 egg, slightly beaten
approximately ½ cup cold water

MEAT FILLING

1 tablespoon butter
1 small onion, minced
1 small garlic clove, crushed
¼ pound beef round, ground twice
¼ pound veal or lean pork, ground twice (see below)

¼ teaspoon salt
⅛ teaspoon freshly ground pepper
1/16 teaspoon Tabasco
clear hot beef consommé
mustard sauce
sour cream
fresh dill

To make the dough, combine flour and salt in a medium-size bowl. With a spoon, make a well in the center of the flour. Add egg and water. Mix thoroughly until mixture clings together, adding a little more water, 1 teaspoon at a time, if necessary. Shape dough into a ball. Turn dough out onto a lightly floured baking board or counter top. Knead lightly for about 1 minute, or until smooth and no longer sticky, adding a little additional flour, 1 teaspoon at a time, if necessary. Place

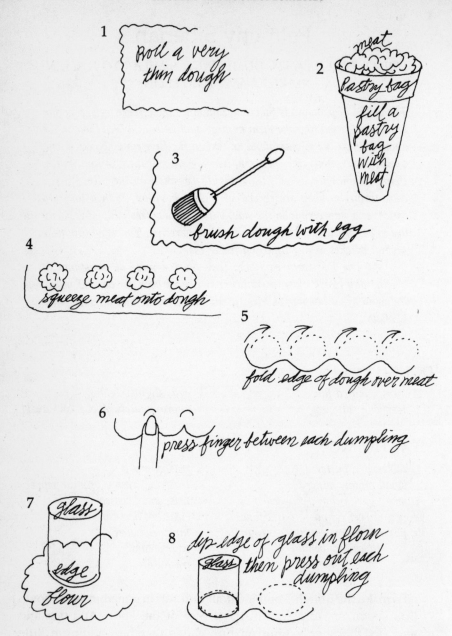

1 Roll a very thin dough

2 meat / Pastry bag / fill a pastry bag with meat

3 brush dough with egg

4 squeeze meat onto dough

5 fold edge of dough over meat

6 press finger between each dumpling

7 glass / edge / flour

8 dip edge of glass in flour then press out each dumpling / glass

dough in a small bowl. Cover with plastic wrap and chill for 1 hour or longer.

Meantime, prepare the Meat Filling. Heat butter in a small frying pan. Add onion and garlic. Cook over medium heat, stirring con-

9

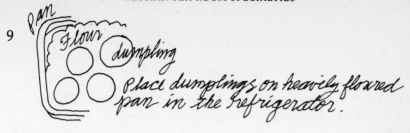

Place dumplings on heavily floured pan in the refrigerator.

stantly, for about 3 to 5 minutes, or until soft. In a small bowl, combine onion mixture, beef, veal or pork, salt, pepper and Tabasco. Mix well; there should be about 1 cup. Divide chilled dough in half, and refrigerate the dough you are not immediately working on. On a lightly floured pastry cloth or other floured surface, and using a stockinette-covered rolling pin, roll the dough into a circle measuring about 16 to 17 inches in diameter and about 1⁄16 inch in thickness. It is essential that the dough be rolled as thin as possible or pelmeny will be too doughy; besides, they swell in the cooking. Using a 2½-inch round cutter, cut out 30 2½-inch circles, rerolling the scraps of dough. Using a rounded ½ teaspoon for each portion, spoon equal amounts of the beef mixture evenly over the lower half of each of the 30 circles. Bring exposed half of the circle up over filling to form 2½- by 1¼-inch crescents. With your fingers, pinch edges together very firmly to seal in filling. Bring the 2 ends (or corners) of each crescent together, pinching them together to form a pouch measuring about 1½ inches. Place the prepared pelmeny in one layer on a platter and cover loosely with a clean kitchen towel. Repeat process with the remaining dough and filling.

In a large soup kettle or Dutch oven bring 3 quarts of water to the boiling point. Drop in about 10 pelmeny. Cook at a rolling boil for about 3 minutes or until done; pelmeny will float to the top of the liquid when cooked, and pork will no longer be pink. Remove with a slotted spoon and drain on paper towels. Repeat with remaining pelmeny. Transfer cooked pelmeny to clear hot beef consommé and heat through. Serve with side dishes of mustard sauce and sour cream, and garnish with fresh dill.

Note: The pelmeny may also be cooked directly in the beef consommé. However, the soup will not be as clear as when the already cooked pelmeny are transferred to the consommé.

Note: To grind your own pork for the ¼ pound specified in the recipe, buy about ½ pound of thin (⅜- to ½-inch) center-cut loin pork chops (about 3 chops). Trim off fat and gristle and remove bone; then grind twice.

Salmon Pojarski

GROUND SALMON PATTIES

In past days, salmon abounded in Russia's northern waters. Grinding it into patties was one of the preferred ways of preparing this noble fish.

Serves 6, 3 patties each

4 *tablespoons butter*
⅓ *cup minced onion*
3 *pounds boned and skinned fresh salmon, ground (see below)*
3 *cups fresh white breadcrumbs*
2 *teaspoons salt*

¼ *teaspoon freshly ground pepper, preferably white*
⅛ *teaspoon ground nutmeg*
1 *cup heavy cream*
3 *tablespoons cooking oil*

Heat 1 tablespoon of the butter in a frying pan. Add onion and cook over medium heat, stirring constantly, for 3 to 5 minutes, or until soft; do not brown. In a large bowl, combine the ground salmon, the onion, ½ cup of the bread crumbs, salt, pepper, nutmeg and heavy cream. Mix thoroughly; mixture will be quite soft. Using a rounded ⅓-cup measure for each portion, divide mixture into 18 equal portions. Shape each portion into oval patties, each measuring 4 by 2 by 1½ inches. (To facilitate shaping, moisten hands with cold water.) Gently and carefully roll patties in the remaining breadcrumbs. Cover and chill for 30 minutes or longer. Heat 1 tablespoon of the remaining butter and 1 tablespoon of the cooking oil in a large (10- or 12-inch), heavy frying pan. Add 6 patties in 1 layer. Cook over medium heat, carefully turning patties 2 or 3 times, for 10 to 12 minutes, or until golden and cooked through. To check for doneness, cut into center of 1 patty. (Longer chilling time may require longer cooking time; if patties are very cold, cook over low heat.) Using a wide spatula, transfer patties to a heated serving platter and keep warm in a low oven (150 to 175°F.). Repeat twice with remaining patties, butter and cooking oil. Serve over a bed of hot rice with a buttered green vegetable and with Fish Velouté Sauce (page 134).

Note: To prepare 3 pounds of boned skinned fresh salmon for grinding, remove skin and bones from about 3½ pounds of salmon steaks.

Blini

THIN BUCKWHEAT PANCAKES, SERVED WITH CAVIAR, SOUR CREAM AND HOT MELTED BUTTER

The ancient Slavic people worshiped the sun, hoping it would return and rescue them from the cold darkness of winter. They recalled the sun's golden image by making Blini, little round pancakes, which they ate to keep warm. The week before the long seven-week Lenten season began was called Myaslanitza, or Butter Week, when everyone gorged on Blini and other dairy products, which they then had to give up until Easter. We still have the Blini Festival every year at The Russian Tea Room to celebrate this winter-solstice event.

Serves 6, 6 blini each

1⅓ cups sifted white flour
1⅓ cups sifted buckwheat flour
4 teaspoons active dry yeast
¼ cup sugar

½ teaspoon salt
2⅔ cups milk
½ cup butter, cut into small pieces
4 eggs, lightly beaten

In a large bowl, combine white flour, buckwheat flour, yeast, sugar and salt. In a small, heavy saucepan, combine milk and butter. Heat mixture over low heat only until milk is warm (105 to 115°F.) and the butter has melted. Stir frequently to speed up the melting of the butter; the milk must not be hotter than the temperature given above. Stir milk mixture into flour mixture and mix well; then stir in the eggs. Using an electric mixer at low speed, beat for about 1 minute or until smooth, occasionally scraping the sides of the bowl. Or do this by hand, beating energetically for 3 to 5 minutes. Cover bowl. Set to rise in a warm place for 1 to 1½ hours, or until mixture is about doubled in volume and light and bubbly. Preheat a griddle or a large (10-inch), heavy (preferably nonstick) frying pan. Lightly brush with a very small amount of melted butter. (Do not use too much, or Blini will turn gray in cooking. The bottom of the griddle or frying pan should be covered with a very light film of butter.) The griddle or frying pan will be hot enough when a drop of water dropped on its surface will evaporate instantly. Stir down batter. To make 4-inch Blini, spoon about 3 tablespoons batter onto the griddle or frying pan. Cook for 40 to 60 seconds, or until the top is bubbly and the bottom browned. Turn over with a large spatula, or flip over, and cook for 30 seconds on the other side or until browned. Stack cooked Blini on a heated serving dish and keep warm in a low oven (150 to 175°F.).

Serve with a bowl of melted butter and a bowl of sour cream at room temperature, and with caviar or smoked fish such as salmon. To eat, brush butter on Blini and top with a small mound of caviar or smoked fish. Top this with a spoonful of sour cream and roll up.

Blinchiki

THIN CREPES FILLED WITH COTTAGE CHEESE, APPLES OR CHERRY PRESERVES, SERVED WITH SOUR CREAM AND POWDERED SUGAR

Our Russian Tea Room guests take strong sides about blinchiki fillings. Purists like pianist Van Cliburn like only apple; others, like Russian dancer and choreographer Mikhail Baryshnikov, like them assorted. But they are much beloved by all.

Serves 6   Makes 18 to 22 crepes

CREPES

2¼ *cups sifted flour*
 ½ *cup sugar*
 ½ *teaspoon salt*
 6 *eggs*
 3 *cups milk*

2 *tablespoons butter, melted*
  few drops of yellow food
    coloring (optional)
  melted butter

Sift flour, sugar and salt together into a large bowl. Beat together eggs, milk, butter and food coloring if you are using it. Stir slowly into flour mixture. With a wire whisk, a rotary beater or an electric beater at low speed, beat until well blended and smooth. Or place flour, sugar, salt, eggs and melted butter into food processor. Start machine and add milk gradually. Scrape down sides. Continue processing until batter is smooth. If time permits, cover batter and let stand at room temperature for 1 to 2 hours. Have ready a small container of melted butter and a small brush. Slowly heat a 6- or 7-inch crepe pan or frying pan until a drop of water dances when dropped on the surface. Brush pan lightly with melted butter. Pour batter, about ¼ cup at a time, into heated pan and quickly rotate the pan to spread the batter evenly. Cook over medium heat until bottom is lightly browned and the top is set. Turn out, browned side up, on a clean kitchen towel or paper towel. Repeat with the remaining batter; if needed, butter the pan lightly between crepes. If you want crisper crepes, brown them on both sides. In that case, stack cooled crepes with wax paper between each until ready to use.

CHEESE FILLING

Makes about 2⅓ cups

1 *pound large-curd cottage or pot cheese, or, preferably, farmer's cheese*	1 *teaspoon vanilla extract*
½ *cup sugar*	3 *tablespoons butter confectioner's sugar*
1 *egg*	1½ *to 2 cups sour cream*

The cheese used for the filling must be very dry or it will ooze out during cooking. Drain cottage or pot cheese for 4 hours before using (farmer's cheese needs no draining). To do this, wrap it in a clean kitchen cloth or in several layers of cheesecloth, tying the ends. Hang over sink to drain; or place unwrapped cheese in a colander, stand the colander in a bowl and top it with a weighted plate to extract moisture. Rub drained cheese through a sieve or a potato ricer for a light, smooth texture. Beat in sugar, egg and vanilla; beat until thoroughly blended. This will fill 18 Blinchiki; freeze remaining crepes for later use.

In the middle of the unbrowned side of each crepe, place about 2 tablespoons of cheese filling. Roll up, jelly-roll fashion, tucking in the ends to cover filling. Heat 1 tablespoon of the butter in a large (10-inch), heavy frying pan. Add 6 filled crepes, in one layer. Heat crepes over moderate heat for about 5 minutes or until the filling is heated through. Turn crepes frequently and carefully to ensure even heating, reducing heat if necessary. Transfer cooked crepes to a warmed serving dish and keep hot in a low oven (150 to 175°F.). Repeat twice with remaining butter and crepes. Sift confectioner's sugar over Blinchiki. Use 3 blinchiki and ¼ to ⅓ cup sour cream for each serving.

APPLE FILLING

Makes about 2¼ cups

1 *one-pound 5-ounce can apple pie filling (about 2¼ cups), drained*	½ *teaspoon ground cinnamon* 18 *crepes*

Combine apple pie filling and cinnamon and mix well. Fill crepes with apples and proceed as for cheese-filled Blinchiki.

CHERRY FILLING

Makes about 2¼ cups

1 *one-pound 5-ounce can cherry pie filling (about 2¼ cups), drained*
18 *crepes*

Fill crepes with cherry filling and proceed as for cheese-filled Blinchiki.

Sirniki

BAKED SWEETENED COTTAGE CHEESE PATTIES SERVED WITH SOUR CREAM AND CONFECTIONER'S SUGAR. THE YOUNGER SISTER OF BLINCHIKI

Serves 6, 3 sirniki each

2 *pounds farmer's cheese*
　　(approximately 4 cups)
2 *egg yolks*
¼ *cup sugar, preferably superfine*

½ *teaspoon salt*
⅔ *cup flour, approximately*
6 *tablespoons butter*
6 *tablespoons cooking oil*

Strain the cheese through a sieve or a food mill; do not use a food processor. In a large bowl, combine the cheese, egg yolks, sugar and salt. Mix thoroughly. Cover the bowl and chill until mixture is firm enough to shape into patties. This will take about 30 minutes in the freezer or approximately 4 hours in the refrigerator. Divide mixture into 2 parts and refrigerate one part until ready to use. Using a scant ¼ cup measure for each portion, divide cheese mixture into 9 portions. Shape each portion into rounds 2 inches in diameter and about ¾ inch high. Handling the patties very carefully and quickly, coat each lightly with a little flour on all sides. Place on a platter and chill for at least 2 hours more. Repeat with remaining cheese mixture and flour. (The long chilling is essential to hold the patties together in cooking.) Remove about 6 patties from the refrigerator and coat once more very lightly with flour. Heat 2 tablespoons each of the butter and oil in a large (10- or 12-inch), heavy frying pan. Place the 6 patties in the pan; they should not touch each other. Cook over medium heat for about 5 minutes or until golden brown. With a spatula, turn over once; if necessary, lower the heat. Transfer to a heated serving dish and keep hot in a low oven (150 to 175°F.). Remove frying pan from heat and clean out with a wad of paper towels. Cook the remaining patties in the remaining butter and oil, cleaning out pan between each batch. (This cleaning out prevents the patties from browning too quickly and too much.) Serve hot, sprinkled with confectioner's sugar and sour cream on the side.

Vareniki
with Cheese Filling, Nut Filling,
Cherry Filling and Sauce

SWEET DESSERT DUMPLINGS SERVED WITH SOUR CREAM AND
CONFECTIONER'S SUGAR

One of Russia's bestloved all-purpose dishes, which lends itself to
many fillings.

Serves 6, 6 vareniki each

DOUGH

2 *cups unsifted flour*
1 *teaspoon salt*

1 *egg, slightly beaten*
½ *cup cold water, approximately*

Combine flour and salt in a medium-size bowl. With a spoon, make a well in the middle of the flour mixture. Add egg and water. Stir with a wooden spoon until mixture clings together. Since flours absorb liquids differently, you may have to add a little more water, 1 tablespoon at a time. Shape into a ball. Turn dough out onto a lightly floured baking board or counter. Knead lightly for about 1 minute, or until smooth and no longer sticky; if necessary, knead in a little more flour, one tablespoon at a time. Place in a small bowl or wrap in waxed paper. Chill for 1 hour or more.

❧❧❧❧❧❧❧

CHEESE FILLING

1 *pound farmer's cheese*
    (approximately 2 cups)
1 *egg yolk*

2 *tablespoons sugar*
¼ *teaspoon salt*

Meanwhile, prepare the Cheese Filling. Strain the farmer's cheese through a sieve or a food mill; do not use a food processor. In a medium-size bowl, combine the cheese, egg yolk, sugar and salt. Mix until thoroughly blended and set aside.

To roll out dough, divide into halves and refrigerate one half. If possible, roll out the dough on a lightly floured pastry cloth, using a stockinette-covered rolling pin; this prevents the dough from absorbing excess flour. Roll out the dough into a circle measuring 16 to 17 inches in diameter and ¹⁄₁₆ inch thick. Using a 3-inch round cutter, cut out 18 3-inch circles, rerolling scraps of dough. Spoon about 1 scant tablespoon of cheese filling onto the lower half of each circle of dough. Bring exposed half of the circle up over the filling to form a 3 by 1½-inch crescent. With fingers, pinch the edges together very firmly to seal in the filling. Cover loosely and set aside. Repeat with remaining dough and filling. Bring 3 quarts of water to the boiling point in a large saucepan or soup kettle. Drop in 10 to 12 dumplings at a time. Cook at a rolling boil for 3 to 5 minutes, or until dumplings float to the top of the water. Remove with a slotted spoon and drain on paper towels. Place on a heated platter and keep warm in a low oven (150 to 175°F.). Repeat until all the dumplings are cooked. Serve with confectioner's sugar and sour cream.

NUT FILLING

Prepare dough as above, but without Cheese Filling. In a medium-size bowl, combine 2 cups ground walnuts (about 1½ cups walnut pieces), ¼ cup honey and ½ teaspoon ground cinnamon. Mix until thoroughly blended. Proceed as above, dividing the Nut Filling among 36 circles of dough and using about 1 packed teaspoon of filling for each circle.

CHERRY FILLING

Prepare dough as above but without Cheese Filling. Drain 2 cans (16 ounces each) pitted sour cherries, and reserve the juice for the Cherry Sauce, below. Using a fork, mash the cherries to a coarse pulp. Add ½ cup sugar to mashed cherries and mix well. Let stand at room temperature for 30 minutes. Drain in a sieve; place cherries in a bowl and reserve the sweetened cherry juice. Drain cherries again on 3 thicknesses of paper towels; cherries must be dry or they will ooze out during cooking. Proceed as above, dividing the Cherry Filling among 36 circles of dough and using about 1 packed teaspoon filling for each circle.

CHERRY SAUCE

Makes 2 cups

Pour ⅔ cup sweetened cherry juice into a 2-cup measure. Add enough reserved unsweetened cherry juice (see above) to equal 2 cups. Pour into a small saucepan and bring to boiling point. Blend 4 tablespoons cornstarch with 4 tablespoons cold water. Stir cornstarch into cherry juice. Cook over low heat, stirring constantly, for 3 to 5 minutes or until clear, thickened and smooth. Remove from heat and stir in 1 tablespoon fresh lemon juice. If a deeper color is desired, stir in 2 or 3 drops of red food coloring. Serve warm over Vareniki with Cherry Filling.

Golubtze

STUFFED CABBAGE ROLLS

All Slavs love this dish because of its sustaining qualities and the mixture of sweet and sour tastes.

Serves 6, 2 rolls each

1 head firm green cabbage (3 pounds)
boiling water
4 tablespoons butter
1 medium onion, minced
1 pound lean ground beef
½ cup raw long-grain rice
1 teaspoon salt
¼ teaspoon freshly ground pepper
¼ teaspoon ground coriander
⅛ teaspoon ground ginger

1 tablespoon fresh lemon juice
⅔ cup golden raisins, plumped in hot water and drained
1 can (1 pound 12 ounces) Italian-style tomatoes (3½ cups)
1 can (1 pound) sauerkraut, rinsed in cold water and drained
1 can (13¾ ounces) beef bouillon (1⅔ cups)

Core the cabbage carefully, leaving head intact. Place in a large kettle. Add enough boiling water to cover the cabbage. Partially cover the kettle with a lid, leaving enough space for steam to escape during cooking. Cook over high heat for about 10 minutes. Carefully lift the cabbage out of the kettle and place it on paper towels. Gently remove 12 outer leaves. Place leaves side by side on paper towels and blot dry. In a large (10- to 12-inch), heavy frying pan, over medium heat, heat the butter. Add the onion and cook, stirring constantly, for 3 to 5 minutes, or until soft and golden; do not brown. Add ground meat, rice, salt, pepper, coriander, ginger, lemon juice and raisins. Mix thoroughly. Cook for 8 to 10 minutes or until meat is browned, breaking the meat up with 2 forks.

Trim center rib off each cabbage leaf at its base. Place about ¼ cup of the meat mixture in the center of each of the 12 cabbage leaves. Roll leaves up and around meat mixture, tucking in sides and ends securely. If the rolls keep on coming apart, tie each with white thread around the middle, or secure them with toothpicks. Place the rolls, seam side down, in a lightly greased 13- by 9- by 2-inch baking pan. Preheat the oven to moderate (350°F.). In a large mixing bowl, combine tomatoes, sauerkraut and beef bouillon and mix thoroughly. Pour the mixture evenly over the cabbage rolls. Cover the baking dish with aluminum foil, tucking it securely around the dish. Bake for about 45 minutes. Remove the foil and bake for 30 more minutes, basting frequently with the pan juices. Serve on a bed of hot cooked rice, with vegetables and the sauce in which the rolls were cooked. Serve Tomato Sauce (page 137) on the side.

Nalistniki

MEAT-STUFFED CREPES

*A favorite dinner dish at The Russian Tea Room, Nalistniki are
served for lunch once a week. The late Paddy Chayefsky loved them.*

Serves 6

12 to 14 crepes

CREPES

1½ cups sifted flour	2 cups milk
¼ teaspoon salt	1½ tablespoons butter, melted
4 eggs	melted butter

Sift flour and salt together into a large bowl. Beat together eggs,
milk and butter. Stir slowly into flour mixture. With a wire whisk, a
rotary beater or an electric beater at low speed, beat until well blended
and smooth. Or place flour, salt, eggs, and melted butter into food
processor. Start machine and add the milk gradually. Scrape down
sides. Continue processing until batter is smooth. If time permits, cover
batter and let stand at room temperature for 1 to 2 hours. Have ready a
small container of melted butter and a small brush. Slowly heat a 6- or
7-inch crepe pan or frying pan until a drop of water evaporates
instantly when dropped on its surface. Brush pan lightly with melted
butter. Pour batter, about ¼ cup at a time, into heated pan and quickly
rotate the pan to spread the batter evenly. Cook over medium heat until
bottom is lightly browned and top is set; turn and lightly brown other
side. Remove to plate. Repeat with remaining batter; if necessary,
butter the pan lightly between crepes. When cool, stack crepes with
wax paper between each until ready to use.

FILLING

6 tablespoons butter	1 pound boned and skinned
1 medium onion, minced	chicken breasts, ground
½ cup minced parsley	(see below)
1 pound lean veal, ground (see	½ cup fine dry breadcrumbs
below)	1 teaspoon salt
	¼ teaspoon freshly ground pepper
	⅛ teaspoon Tabasco sauce

Heat 2 tablespoons of the butter in a large (10-inch) heavy frying pan. Add onion and parsley. Cook over medium heat, stirring constantly, for about 5 minutes, or until onion is soft and golden. Add ground veal and chicken. Cook 5 to 7 minutes, stirring frequently, until meats are golden brown and cooked. Stir in breadcrumbs, salt, pepper and Tabasco and mix well. Cool mixture.

On each of the 12 (or 14) crepes, place about ⅓ cup of filling, pushing it toward the end of the crepe and firming it lightly with your fingers to keep the filling from falling out during cooking. Roll crepes up jelly-roll fashion. Secure rolled crepes with toothpicks or kitchen thread. Heat 2 tablespoons of the remaining butter in a large heavy frying pan. Add 6 or 7 filled crepes, in one layer. Heat crepes over moderate heat for 8 to 10 minutes, or until the filling is heated through. Turn crepes frequently and carefully to ensure even heating, lowering heat if necessary. Transfer cooked crepes to a warmed serving dish and keep hot in a low oven (150 to 175°F.). Repeat with remaining butter and crepes. Or place filled crepes, seam side down, in a single layer and close together in a buttered baking dish. Bake without a cover in a medium oven (350°F.) for about 20 minutes, or until heated through. Serve with Brown or Espagnole Sauce (page 130).

Notes: The filling may also be prepared with 2 pounds of ground beef. Or use any leftover Pojarski Cutlets, ground fine.

To prepare 1 pound lean veal for grinding, you will need 1½ pounds of boneless veal shoulder, since all fat and gristle must be trimmed off the meat. Use food processor for grinding, or push twice through a meat grinder.

To prepare 1 pound uncooked boned and skinned chicken breasts for grinding, remove bones, fat and skin from 2 pounds chicken breasts; or remove skin and fat from 4 boneless chicken cutlets, total weight approximately 1 pound. Use food processor for grinding, or push twice through meat grinder.

Mushrooms à la Russe

*FRESH MUSHROOMS IN CASSEROLE, AU GRATIN, BAKED IN A
MUSHROOM SAUCE. THE MUSHROOMS MUST BE FIRM, WHITE,
AND VERY FRESH, WITH CLOSED CAPS*

*This dish is closely associated with Carnegie Hall, as it is a favorite of
concert-goers who want something tasty and nourishing before they
dash next door. If Isaac Stern is playing he may come in early to enjoy
it en famille.*

Serves 6

3 *to 4 quarts water*	1 *cup sour cream*
2 *tablespoons salt*	1 *teaspoon salt or to taste*
2 *pounds mushrooms*	½ *teaspoon freshly ground pepper*
6 *tablespoons butter*	*or to taste*
½ *cup minced onion (1 medium-*	¼ *teaspoon Worcestershire sauce*
size onion)	¼ *teaspoon ground coriander*
⅓ *cup flour*	½ *cup grated Parmesan cheese*
1 *cup milk*	

Combine water and salt in a large kettle and bring to the boiling
point. Meanwhile, trim mushrooms, place in a bowl and wash quickly
but thoroughly under running water, swishing them around with the
hands. Drain mushrooms and put them into the boiling water. Cook
over medium heat for no more than 2 minutes after water has resumed
boiling. Drain in a colander. Place drained mushrooms stem side down
on a platter lined with 3 thicknesses of paper towels to drain further.
Pat dry with more paper towels; they must be as dry as possible or dish
will be soupy. Cool mushrooms and slice thin. Reserve.

Heat butter in a large (10- to 12-inch) deep frying pan or a shallow
saucepan such as a *sauteuse*. Add onion. Cook over medium heat,
stirring constantly, for 3 to 5 minutes, or until soft; do not brown. Add
mushrooms. Cook, stirring all the time, for 3 to 4 minutes. Sprinkle
with the flour, toss well and cook for 2 more minutes. Combine milk
and sour cream in a small saucepan, and heat, stirring; do not boil. Add
to the mushrooms and mix thoroughly. Remove from heat and stir in
salt, pepper, Worcestershire sauce and ground coriander. Turn into 6
individual baking dishes or into a 10- to 12-cup baking dish. Sprinkle
with the Parmesan. Cook in a preheated moderate oven (350°F.) for 20
minutes or until golden brown and bubbly. Serve hot.

Eggplant à la Russe

EGGPLANT IN CASSEROLE BAKED WITH CREAM AND SOUR CREAM—A VEGETARIAN'S DELIGHT

Serves 6

2 *eggplants, each weighing approximately 1 pound*
3 *quarts water*
2 *tablespoons salt*
4 *tablespoons butter*
¼ *cup minced onion*
½ *cup flour*
1 *cup milk*
1 *cup heavy cream*
1 *teaspoon salt*

½ *teaspoon freshly ground pepper, preferably white*
1 *to 1½ teaspoons prepared mustard, preferably Dijon*
¼ *teaspoon ground coriander*
½ *teaspoon paprika*
½ *cup sour cream*
6 *tablespoons grated Parmesan cheese*

Trim and peel eggplants and cut into ½-inch cubes. Combine water and salt in a large kettle and bring to the boiling point. Add eggplant. Cook for no more than 3 minutes after water has resumed boiling. Drain thoroughly; this is important or the dish will be soupy. Heat the butter in a large, heavy frying pan. Add the onion. Cook over medium heat, stirring constantly, for 3 to 5 minutes, or until onion is tender; do not brown. Turn heat to low. Stir in flour and cook, stirring all the time, for 2 to 3 minutes, but do not brown. Stir in milk and cream. Cook, stirring constantly, until sauce is smooth and thickened. Stir in salt, pepper, mustard, coriander and paprika and cook for 2 or 3 more minutes. Remove from heat and stir sour cream into sauce. Check the seasoning, remembering that eggplant is on the bland side. Turn eggplant into a 10- or 12-cup baking dish, or into 6 individual baking dishes. Spoon all the sauce over the eggplant in the large baking dish, or divide it among the 6 individual ones. Sprinkle with Parmesan cheese. Cook in a hot oven (400°F.) for 10 to 15 minutes, or until top is bubbly and brown. Serve hot.

Mussáka

Mussáka is a three-layer casserole that takes a little time to assemble but makes an excellent party and buffet dish. It is served in all countries around the Mediterranean and the Black Sea, including Greece, Turkey and the Ukraine and the Caucasus in Russia.

Serves 8 to 10

BOTTOM LAYER

4 medium eggplants (each weighing about ¾ to 1 pound)

salt (2 to 3 tablespoons)
¼ cup fine dry breadcrumbs
about ⅔ cup olive oil

MIDDLE LAYER

4 tablespoons butter
3 medium onions, minced
2 pounds lean ground beef or lamb
1½ cups finely chopped tomatoes, or ¼ cup tomato paste, or ¾ cup tomato sauce
¼ cup minced parsley
½ cup dry white or red wine

½ teaspoon oregano
½ cup water
¼ teaspoon ground cinnamon
2 teaspoons salt
¼ teaspoon freshly ground pepper
3 eggs, beaten
¼ cup fine dry breadcrumbs
½ cup grated Parmesan cheese

TOP LAYER

6 tablespoons butter
6 tablespoons flour
3⅓ cups hot milk
1 teaspoon salt
¼ teaspoon freshly ground pepper (preferably white)

⅛ teaspoon ground nutmeg
4 egg yolks, lightly beaten
¼ cup grated Parmesan cheese

Wash eggplants and cut off stem ends. With a sharp knife or a vegetable peeler, remove 1½-inch-wide strips of peel lengthwise from eggplants, leaving ½ inch of peel between the strips. (This will prevent eggplant from disintegrating when fried later.) Cut eggplants into ¼-inch round slices. Place slices on 1 or 2 large platters in 2 or 3 layers, sprinkling each layer with a little of the salt. Top platters with other platters or plates and weigh down with filled cans of food, or canisters of flour or sugar—the heavier the better. Let stand at room temperature for 1 to 2 hours to release the bitter juice. Drop eggplant slices into a bowl with cold water to wash off salt and juice. Drain and pat dry with paper towels; slices must be thoroughly dry.

Meanwhile, butter a 14- by 10- by 2-inch baking pan that can also go to the table. Sprinkle bottom and sides with the breadcrumbs. Start making meat sauce for Middle Layer.

In a large (10- to 12-inch) heavy frying pan or shallow saucepan, over medium heat, heat the butter. Add onions and cook, stirring constantly, for about 3 to 5 minutes, or until soft and golden; do not brown. Add the meat and, breaking up chunks with 2 forks, cook for 10 to 15 minutes or until browned. Turn heat to low. Add the tomatoes or tomato paste or tomato sauce, the parsley, wine, oregano, salt and pepper. (If you have used tomato paste, add the ½ cup water.) Cook, uncovered, stirring frequently, for about 15 minutes, or until liquid is absorbed. Cool. Stir in cinnamon, eggs, breadcrumbs and Parmesan cheese. Blend thoroughly.

Now, fry the drained, dried eggplant slices. Add about 3 or 4 tablespoons of olive oil to a large frying pan; if frying pan is large, add about 4 tablespoons. Heat the oil to medium-hot, but do not let it smoke. Over medium heat, add eggplant slices in one layer. Brown slices quickly on both sides. Drain on paper towels. Continue until all the eggplant slices are fried, adding olive oil as needed and draining each batch on paper towels as done. Using about half of the fried eggplant slices, line the bottom of the baking pan, overlapping rounds and fitting them closely together. Spread the meat sauce evenly over the eggplant. Top with remaining eggplant slices, fitting them closely as well. (At this point, recipe can be prepared ahead of time and refrigerated. Bring to room temperature before finishing the Mussáka.)

Now make the sauce for the Top Layer. Preheat oven to low (325°F.). Heat the butter in a heavy saucepan. Stir in flour and, over low heat, cook for about 2 minutes, stirring constantly. Do not let flour brown. Add milk. Cook, stirring all the while, until sauce is thickened and smooth. Stir in salt and pepper and cook for 2 more minutes. Remove from heat and stir in nutmeg. Combine beaten egg yolks with a little of the sauce and add to the rest of sauce in the pan. Stir in Parmesan. Return to very low heat and cook, stirring constantly, for about 2 minutes. Do not let sauce boil. Remove from heat and cool to room temperature.

Spread sauce evenly over top eggplant layer. Bake Mussáka, uncovered, for 1 to 1½ hours, or until topping is golden and slightly puffy. Remove from oven and let stand for 10 minutes at room temperature. Cut into squares for serving. Serve with Cucumber Salad (page 165).

Baked Ham with Cherry Sauce

We serve this festive dish at Easter and other holidays, and for private parties.

Serves 12 to 14

1 12- to 14-pound smoked ham, processed, precooked
1 cup brown sugar
⅓ cup honey

1 tablespoon dry mustard, or 2 tablespoons sharp Dijon mustard
20 whole cloves (approximately)

BASTING SAUCE

1 cup brown sugar
1 teaspoon dry mustard, or 1 tablespoon Dijon mustard
1 cup cherry juice

Preheat the oven to low (325°F.). Set a rack in a shallow baking pan large enough to hold the ham comfortably. Place the ham, fat side up, on the rack. Bake for 2 hours without basting, 10 to 15 minutes per pound, or until the meat is tender. About 45 minutes before the ham is done, remove it from the oven. Place the ham on a board and cut away the rind and most of the fat with a large, sharp knife. Score the remaining fat on the ham in a diamond pattern, cutting deeply until you reach the meat. Combine the brown sugar, honey and mustard and mix well. Spread mixture over the ham. Place whole cloves in the center of each scored diamond on the ham's surface. Return the ham to the rack in the pan, and return to oven.

Make the Basting Sauce by mixing the brown sugar, mustard and cherry juice. Bake the ham for 45 to 60 minutes more, basting it every 10 minutes with the basting sauce. Turn off the oven and let the ham rest for 15 minutes before placing on a platter and carving at the table. Serve Chunky Cherry Sauce (page 128) on the side.

Accompaniments and Sauces

Boiled Potatoes with Sour Cream

ROUND REDS, THOSE TASTY VERY LITTLE NEW POTATOES, ARE BEST FOR THIS, ESPECIALLY IN THE SPRING

Serves 4

2 pounds little new potatoes in their skins (8 to 16, depending on size), scrubbed

boiling water
2 teaspoons salt
2 cups sour cream

Place potatoes in a large saucepan. Add boiling water to cover about 4 inches above potatoes. Stir in the salt. Cook, covered, over medium heat for 10 to 15 minutes, or until tender but not mushy. Drain, return to saucepan and quickly shake dry over direct heat. Turn into a serving dish lined with a napkin and cover with the napkin to keep hot. Serve with a bowl of sour cream on the side.

Rice Pilaff

Since rice accompanies so many of our main dishes, especially those made with lamb, we are naturally eager to cook it as beautifully as possible. We find that one of the most popular rice dishes is Pilaff—rice cooked in chicken consommé for a specific number of minutes. Pilaff, which comes from the Middle East, is easy and foolproof, but attention should be paid to the fact that the two best-known kinds of rice, regular, or long-grain, and converted (Uncle Ben is the best-known brand) are cooked with different amounts of liquid for different amounts of time. Whatever the rice, you will need a pot with a really tight lid.

Serves 4 to 5

6 tablespoons butter	½ teaspoon salt
1 cup long-grain rice	¼ teaspoon freshly ground pepper
1¾ cups chicken consommé	

Heat 2 tablespoons of the butter in a heavy 2- to 3-quart saucepan with a tight-fitting lid. Cut the remaining butter into small pieces and reserve. Add the rice to the pan. Cook over medium heat, stirring constantly with a wooden spoon, for 2 to 3 minutes or until the rice begins to turn opaque. Do not brown the rice. Add the chicken consommé, salt and pepper. Bring to the boiling point, stirring constantly. Cover the saucepan tightly and turn heat down as low as possible. Cook for 12 to 15 minutes without stirring or until all the liquid has been absorbed. The rice should be tender but not mushy. Stir the remaining butter into the rice. Remove from the heat and let stand, covered, for 5 minutes. Serve immediately.

CONVERTED RICE

To 1 cup converted rice, use 2¼ cups of chicken consommé. Proceed as for regular long-grain rice, but cook for 20 minutes. Remove from the heat and let stand, covered, for 5 minutes. Serve immediately.
Note: This recipe can be easily doubled or tripled.

Georgian Rice Pilaff

A SAVORY MAIN DISH THAT CONTAINS NO MEAT

Serves 6 to 8

⅓ cup butter
3 medium onions, finely chopped
⅓ cup coarsely chopped walnuts or
    whole pine nuts (pignoli)
⅓ cup currants or golden raisins,
    plumped in hot water and
    drained
2 cups converted rice
4 cups hot chicken consommé

2 large tomatoes, skinned, seeded
    and coarsely chopped
¼ cup minced parsley
1 teaspoon ground sage
½ teaspoon ground coriander
¼ teaspoon ground cinnamon
    salt
    freshly ground pepper

Heat the butter in a large, heavy saucepan. Add the onions and cook over medium heat, stirring constantly, for 3 to 4 minutes or until soft and golden; do not brown. Add the nuts and the currants or raisins and cook, stirring all the time, for 1 more minute. Add the rice. Cook, stirring constantly, for about 3 to 4 minutes, or until the rice begins to turn opaque. Add the remaining ingredients, except salt and pepper, and mix thoroughly. Taste for seasoning and add salt and pepper to taste. Bring to the boiling point and immediately lower the heat to very low. Cover tightly and cook for about 20 minutes or until the rice is tender but still firm. Remove from heat and remove the cover. Place a clean kitchen towel over the rice and cover again. Let stand for 5 minutes; the towel will absorb any remaining moisture from the rice. Serve with Ogurtze Salad (page 164).

Note: This recipe can be easily doubled or tripled, provided you have a large enough saucepan.

Kasha

ONE OF THE MAINSTAYS OF THE RUSSIAN DIET, MADE OF BUCKWHEAT GRAINS, OR GROATS (CRACKED KERNELS)

Kasha serves as a delicious substitute for potatoes, pasta and rice in Russia. Cooked mushrooms, fried onions, cooked bits of meat or chicken, all may be added to cooked kasha for an attractive, nutritious main dish. Packaged kasha is available in supermarkets. If there is a choice between fine and coarse kasha, choose the latter for best results.

Serves 4 to 6

1 egg
1 cup coarse kasha (buckwheat groats)
¼ cup butter, cut into pieces

2 cups chicken or beef consommé or water
¾ teaspoon salt
¼ teaspoon freshly ground pepper

Lightly beat the egg in a small bowl. Add the kasha. Toss together with a wooden spoon, making sure that all the grains are coated with egg. Transfer to a large (10- to 12-inch) frying pan. Cook over moderate heat, stirring constantly with a wooden spoon, until the kasha is lightly toasted and dried out. Do not burn. Add the remaining ingredients and mix well. Turn heat to low and cover the frying pan tightly. Simmer for about 15 minutes. Stir occasionally. If the kasha has absorbed all the liquid but is not yet tender, add a little hot water, 2 tablespoons at a time. (Be sure not to cook until mushy.) The grains of the cooked kasha should be separate. Fluff with a fork, check the seasonings and serve hot.

MUSHROOM KASHA

4 tablespoons butter
1 cup finely chopped onion

1 recipe hot Kasha (see above)
½ pound coarsely chopped mushrooms.

Heat 2 tablespoons of the butter in a heavy frying pan. Add the onion and cook over medium heat, stirring constantly, for 3 to 5 minutes, or until tender; do not brown. Stir the onions into the kasha and keep hot in a low oven (150 to 175°F.). Add the remaining butter to the same frying pan. When melted, add the mushrooms. Cook over medium heat, stirring constantly, for about 5 minutes, or until soft but still firm. Stir into the kasha. Check the seasonings and serve hot.

Chunky Cherry Sauce

Makes about 3 cups

2 *cups dry white wine*
½ *medium-size onion, chopped*
2 *garlic cloves, chopped*
3 *bay leaves*
½ *teaspoon dried thyme*
3 *tablespoons butter*
2 *tablespoons minced onion*
1 *garlic clove, minced*
½ *cup cherry juice*
⅛ *teaspoon dried thyme*
¼ *teaspoon ground coriander*

¼ *teaspoon ground ginger*
½ *teaspoon salt*
⅛ *teaspoon cayenne pepper*
1 *teaspoon Dijon mustard*
   grated rind of 1 large orange
   grated rind of 1 lemon
2 *cups whole pitted drained sweet*
      canned cherries, chopped
1 *tablespoon Madeira or brandy*
1 *tablespoon butter, cut into*
      pieces

In a medium-size saucepan, combine the dry white wine, the chopped onion, the 2 garlic cloves, the bay leaves and thyme. Cook, uncovered, over high heat for about 10 minutes, or until the liquid is reduced to about half its original amount. Drain. The wine should be reduced to about 1 cup. Reserve. Heat the 3 tablespoons of butter in a saucepan and add the 2 tablespoons minced onion and the minced garlic clove. Cook over low heat for about 4 minutes or until soft; do not brown. Stir in the reserved wine, cherry juice, thyme, coriander, ginger, salt, cayenne, mustard, orange rind and lemon rind. Cook, uncovered, over medium heat for 10 minutes. Add the chopped cherries and cook for 5 to 10 minutes more; the cherries should remain chunky. You can use a processor to chop the cherries, but take care not to overprocess or the cherries will be puréed. Check the seasoning; the sauce should taste subtly of coriander, ginger and garlic. Stir in Madeira or brandy and remove from heat. Stir in the tablespoon of butter and serve hot.

Sauce Stroganoff

Makes 2⅓ cups

4 tablespoons butter
2 tablespoons minced onion
¼ cup flour
2 cups milk
½ teaspoon salt
⅛ teaspoon freshly ground white
    pepper

¼ teaspoon Tabasco sauce
½ teaspoon prepared mustard,
    preferably Dijon
⅛ teaspoon ground coriander
⅓ cup sour cream, warmed

Heat 1 tablespoon of the butter in a small frying pan. Add the onion and cook over low heat, stirring constantly, for 2 to 3 minutes, or until soft but still white. In the top of a double boiler, over direct low heat, heat the remaining butter. Stir in flour and cook for 2 minutes. Add the milk, salt and pepper. Cook, stirring constantly, until the sauce is smooth and thickened. Stir in onion, Tabasco, mustard and coriander. Set double boiler top over simmering water. Cover and cook over low heat, keeping water at a simmer, for 45 minutes. (This long, slow cooking is necessary to remove the taste of uncooked flour.) Stir the sauce occasionally, scraping down the bottom and sides of the double boiler top with a rubber spatula. Stir in the sour cream. Cook for 5 more minutes, or until heated through; do not boil. Serve hot. Served with Bitochki.

Sauce Espagnole
(Basic Brown Sauce)

This is a classic French sauce and the foundation of many other sauces, such as our Mushroom Sauce (page 132). It is called "Spanish" sauce because it is dark, and because the French who named it thought it resembled the color of many a Spaniard's complexion. But the sauce has no connection with Spanish cooking. It is impossible to make it in small quantities, but it freezes well and will add elegance to any dish that calls for a brown sauce.

Makes 2 quarts

5 *pounds veal bones*
2 *teaspoons salt*
1 *teaspoon freshly ground pepper*
2 *medium onions, coarsely*
   chopped
2 *medium carrots, coarsely*
   chopped
2 *celery stalks, coarsely chopped*
½ *cup flour*
3 *quarts water*

1 *cup tomato sauce*
1 *cup medium-dry sherry or*
   Madeira
1 *leek, white and green parts,*
   chopped (about 1 cup)
1 *cup parsley sprigs*
4 *garlic cloves, mashed*
4 *bay leaves*
1 *teaspoon dried thyme*

Preheat the oven to hot (450°F.). Wash the bones and dry them with paper towels. Spread the bones in a large shallow baking pan in one layer. Sprinkle with the salt and pepper. Add the onions, carrots and celery. Roast the bones for about 1 hour, or until browned. (Reduce the heat to moderate (350°F.) as necessary, to prevent the bones from burning.) Turn the bones once, when they are beginning to brown. Sprinkle them with the flour, toss bones and vegetables together and roast for another 15 minutes. The bones must be dark brown, but not burned.

Place all the bones and vegetables in a very large soup kettle. Add 2 to 3 cups of the water to the roasting pan. Cook over medium heat for 3 to 5 minutes or until the water boils, stirring constantly and scraping up the brown bits at the bottom of the pan. Pour this liquid into the soup kettle with the bones. Add the remaining water, the tomato sauce, the wine, leek, parsley sprigs, garlic cloves, bay leaves and thyme. Bring quickly to the boiling point, turn heat to very low, and simmer, covered, for 2 hours. Skim frequently to remove fat and foam that will rise to the top. Cool the sauce and strain it into a bowl. Discard bones and vegetables. Cover sauce with plastic wrap and chill. Remove any congealed fat from the surface. Use sauce as needed and freeze the rest.

Note: There should be approximately 2 quarts of strained sauce. If there is much more, turn all the sauce into a clean saucepan, place over high heat and reduce it to 2 quarts or thereabouts.

Mushroom Sauce

Makes about 2 cups

2 *tablespoons butter*
1 *tablespoon minced shallots or*
    onion
¼ *pound mushrooms, thinly sliced*

1½ *cups Basic Brown Sauce (Sauce*
      Espagnole) (see page 130)
½ *cup dry Madeira*
      salt
      freshly ground pepper

Heat the butter in a shallow saucepan or a deep frying pan. Add the shallots or onion and the mushrooms. Cook over low heat, stirring frequently, for about 5 minutes. Add the Basic Brown Sauce and the Madeira and mix well. Check the seasoning; if necessary, add salt and pepper to taste. Bring to the boiling point and remove immediately from the heat. Serve very hot. Good with London Broil and other meats.

Madeira Sauce

Makes about 2 cups

1 *tablespoon butter*
1 *tablespoon minced shallots or*
    onion
1⅔ *cups Basic Brown Sauce (page*
      130)

⅓ *cup dry Madeira*
2 *tablespoons lemon juice*

Heat the butter in a saucepan. Add the shallots or onion. Cook over low heat, stirring constantly, for 3 to 4 minutes, or until soft; do not brown the butter. Add the Basic Brown Sauce and the Madeira. Cook over low heat for 4 to 5 minutes. Stir in the lemon juice and remove from the heat. Serve hot. Good with Shashlik Caucasian, Karsky Shashlik, Roast Leg of Lamb and other meats.

Sauce Bechamel

Makes 2⅓ cups

4 *tablespoons butter*
¼ *cup flour*
½ *teaspoon salt*
¼ *teaspoon freshly ground white
     pepper*

⅓ *teaspoon ground nutmeg*
1 *cup milk*
1 *cup heavy cream*
2 *to 3 tablespoons sour cream*

Heat the butter in a heavy saucepan, or, preferably, in the top of a double boiler. Set either over direct low heat and stir in flour, salt, pepper and nutmeg. Cook, stirring constantly, for about 2 minutes or until blended; the mixture must remain as light in color as possible. Gradually stir in the milk and cream. Cook, stirring constantly, until the sauce is smooth and thickened. Set saucepan over lowest possible heat (over a flame tamer), or, if using the double boiler, set the top over simmering water. Cover and cook over low heat (or over simmering water) for 30 to 45 minutes. (The long, slow cooking removes the raw taste of the flour.) Stir the sauce occasionally; scrape bottom and sides of double boiler top with a rubber spatula. Stir in sour cream and cook for 1 more minute; do not boil. Serve hot.

SHERRY BECHAMEL

After the sauce has been removed from the heat, stir in 1 to 2 tablespoons dry or medium sherry, or to taste.

Chicken Velouté Sauce

Makes about 2¼ cups

6 *tablespoons butter*
6 *tablespoons flour*
2 *cups chicken consommé*
    salt

freshly ground pepper
⅛ *teaspoon nutmeg (optional)*
2 *tablespoons sour cream, at room*
    temperature

Heat the butter in a heavy saucepan over moderate heat. Stir in the flour and cook, stirring constantly, for 1 to 2 minutes; do not brown. Stir in the chicken consommé. Cook over low heat, stirring constantly, until the sauce is thick and smooth. Add salt and pepper to taste; go easy on the salt, as the consommé may be salty. Stir in the nutmeg if you are using it. Remove from the heat and stir in the sour cream. Serve hot.

FISH VELOUTÉ SAUCE

Proceed as above, but substitute Fish Stock or clam juice for the consommé and omit the nutmeg.

Fish Stock

USE FOR FISH VELOUTÉ SAUCE

Makes about 2 quarts

2 *pounds bones and heads of any*
    white fish
2 *quarts water*
1 *cup dry white wine*

3 *parsley sprigs*
1 *teaspoon dried thyme*
1 *bay leaf*
1 *teaspoon salt or to taste*

Wash the fish bones and heads in several changes of water. Drain. Place in a large saucepan or kettle and add all the remaining ingredients. (Go easy on the salt; the dishes for which this fish stock will be used will also call for salt.) Bring to the boiling point, cover and simmer over very low heat for 30 to 60 minutes. Strain through a triple layer of fine cheesecloth or through a fine sieve. Cool the stock before using it in sauces or for poaching fish.

Note: This stock freezes well. It may be kept, tightly covered, preferably in a glass container, in the refrigerator for about a week.

Horseradish Sauce

Makes about 2 cups

4 *tablespoons butter*
4 *tablespoons flour*
1 *cup hot milk or half and half*
1¼ *cups hot chicken bouillon*
½ *teaspoon salt*

¼ *teaspoon freshly ground pepper (preferably white)*
¼ *to ⅓ cup prepared horseradish, drained*

Over low heat, melt butter in a heavy saucepan or in the top of a double boiler. Stir in flour and cook, stirring all the time, for 1 to 2 minutes; do not brown. Add milk, chicken bouillon, salt and pepper. Cook over low heat, or, if using double boiler, over simmering hot water, stirring constantly, until sauce is thickened and smooth. Place a flame tamer over heat to make it as low as possible. Cover the saucepan or double boiler top and cook for 10 more minutes, stirring occasionally. This will remove the raw taste of the flour; sauce may be cooked up to 40 minutes. (If sauce becomes too thick with long cooking, stir in a little hot milk or chicken bouillon, 1 tablespoon at a time.) When ready to serve, stir horseradish into sauce and cook, stirring constantly, for 3 more minutes. Serve hot.

Easy Creamy Horseradish Sauce

We serve this sauce with our Boiled Beef Tongue, but it is just as good with Salmon or with Chicken Pojarski. Or, for that matter, with any dish that requires a sharp, creamy sauce. The amount of horseradish can be adjusted to suit your personal taste. The recipe may be halved or doubled.

Makes about 2 cups

2 tablespoons butter
½ cup (or to taste) freshly grated
      horseradish, or drained
      bottled horseradish

1 quart heavy cream
   salt
   freshly ground white pepper

Heat the butter in a large heavy saucepan. Add the horseradish. Cook over low heat, stirring constantly, for 2 or 3 minutes. Add the cream. Cook over low to medium heat, stirring frequently, until the sauce has cooked down to about half of its original amount and has thickened. Take care not to let the sauce boil over or to scorch. Remove from heat and season with salt and pepper to taste. Pour into a heated sauceboat. For a smoother sauce, strain before pouring into the sauceboat. Serve very hot.

Tomato Sauce from Fresh Tomatoes

The quick cooking of the tomatoes preserves a fresh flavor. The yield indicated here depends on the juiciness and ripeness of the tomatoes.

Makes 3 to 5 cups

3 pounds ripe plum tomatoes, cut into halves and seeded, or 3 cups drained canned Italian-style plum tomatoes plus 1 cup of their juice (these will taste fresh if cooked quickly)
1 medium onion, cut in half
1 medium carrot, minced

½ celery stalk, minced
salt
freshly ground pepper
2 to 3 tablespoons fresh basil or fresh coriander, minced, or 1 teaspoon dried basil leaves, or ½ teaspoon ground coriander
⅓ cup olive or salad oil

In a heavy saucepan, combine the tomatoes, half the onion, the carrot, celery, a little salt and pepper and the basil or coriander. Bring quickly to the boiling point. Cook over high heat, stirring constantly, for 4 to 5 minutes, or just until the tomatoes are soft; the riper, the less cooking time required. Purée through a food mill (a food processor will not do because it will not separate skins and seeds from the pulp). Finely chop the remaining onion half. Heat the olive oil in a heavy saucepan and cook, stirring constantly, for 2 minutes, or until soft but not browned. Add puréed tomatoes. Check the seasoning and add, if necessary, more salt and pepper. Cook over medium heat, stirring frequently, for 10 minutes—no longer—to preserve the fresh tomato flavor.

ENTREES

At The Russian Tea Room, you don't have to eat Russian if you don't feel like it. Many of our guests, especially those who come practically every day, want a change of cuisine every now and then. Since we agree with them that variety is the spice of life, our menu features quite a number of dishes of general American appeal. They are a change of pace from the Russian specialties, for those who have other tastes, too. Or they may be combined with one or two Russian specialties, such as zakuska, a soup or a dessert.

We have found that combining American with Russian Tea Room specialties works very well for an international clientele.

The recipes that follow are the American specialties most asked for and served at The Russian Tea Room.

London Broil

A DELICIOUS, STRAIGHTFORWARD DISH FOR THOSE WHO HAVE DINED ON RUSSIAN SPECIALTIES FOR THE PAST SIX DAYS AND WANT TO REST

For tender London Broil, cook it rare and cut it across the grain in thin slices.

Serves 6

one 2½- to 3-pound flank steak
1 cup salad oil
⅓ cup fresh lemon juice
1 teaspoon salt
½ teaspoon freshly ground pepper
⅓ cup chopped onion
1 large garlic clove, minced
2 bay leaves
½ teaspoon dried thyme

Trim all excess fat from the flank steak. Score the steak on both sides, making a criss-cross pattern of cuts ⅛ inch deep and 1 inch apart. (These cuts help the steak tenderize in the marinade and the broiling.) Combine all the remaining ingredients in a large bowl; do not use aluminum. Mix thoroughly. Add meat and turn several times to coat it on all sides with the marinade. Cover with plastic wrap and refrigerate for 6 hours or overnight, turning once.

Preheat broiler. Drain meat and reserve marinade. Broil on an oiled rack about 3 inches from the source of heat for 4 minutes. Baste with reserved marinade once. Turn with tongs and broil 4 more minutes. Transfer to a heated platter (preferably a board or platter with a well to allow juices to collect). If desired, season with salt and pepper to taste. With a slight slant to the carving knife, carve across the grain into ⅛- to ¼-inch-thick slices. Spoon meat juices over slices and serve hot. Serve over a bed of hot cooked rice with a vegetable and Mushroom Sauce (page 132) on the side.

Braised Short Ribs of Beef, Horseradish Sauce

This was introduced to please the palate of that intrepid Englishman, James Stewart-Gordon (sportsman, game-hunter and bon vivant).

Serves 6

3½ *pounds short ribs of beef, cut into 6 pieces*
¼ *cup flour*
1 *teaspoon salt*
¼ *teaspoon freshly ground pepper*
2 *tablespoons salad oil*

2 *medium onions, thinly sliced*
1 *can (1 pound 12 ounces) Italian-style tomatoes, or about 3½ cups*
1 *cup dry red wine*

Preheat oven to moderate (350°F.). Trim most fat off the meat. Combine flour, salt and pepper and sprinkle over ribs, coating meat well on all sides. Heat salad oil in a large (12-inch) heavy frying pan. Add ribs. Cook over moderate heat for 10 to 15 minutes, browning the ribs slowly and turning them occasionally to brown on all sides. Transfer browned ribs to a large casserole or Dutch oven. Pour all fat from the frying pan except 2 tablespoons. Add onions and cook, stirring constantly, for 5 to 7 minutes, or until soft and golden. Add onions, tomatoes and wine to ribs in the casserole. Bake, covered, for 1½ to 2 hours, or until the meat is tender. If the sauce is too thin, bake without a cover for the last 30 minutes, or until it reaches desired consistency. Skim any fat off the sauce. Place ribs in a heated deep platter and spoon sauce over the meat. Serve with boiled potatoes and Horseradish Sauce (page 135).

Noisette of Spring Lamb

Makes 6 slices

2   *pounds lean boneless lamb*   8   *tablespoons butter*
1½ *teaspoons salt*   ⅓   *cup brandy*
¼   *teaspoon freshly ground pepper*

Trim any fat and gristle off the meat. Cut into ¼-inch-thick slices. Place slices side by side between 2 layers of wax paper. With a mallet or a rolling pin, pound into ¼-inch thickness. Trim lamb slices to even sizes. Sprinkle salt and pepper evenly over the meat. In a large, heavy frying pan, over medium heat, heat the butter but do not let it brown. Add lamb slices in 1 layer. Cook for 2 minutes; turn and cook for 1 more minute. Do not overcook—the meat must just be browned. Transfer to a heated serving dish and keep warm in a low oven (150 to 175°F.). When all the meat has been cooked, add brandy, and, scraping up all the brown bits from the bottom of the frying pan, bring pan juices to the boiling point. Cook for 1 minute and pour over meat. Serve in a border of hot cooked rice, with vegetables on the side, and with Mushroom Sauce (page 132), or Madeira Sauce (page 132).

Vienna Schnitzel

Vienna Schnitzel has always been a favorite at The Russian Tea Room. Veal is rarely seen in Russian cuisine aside from cotelettes, but this was borrowed, like the Sacher Torte, from Vienna. In order to have a golden-brown, crisp cutlet, prepare the meat just before cooking. If the prepared schnitzel is allowed to stand, or is refrigerated, the crumbs will be moistened and turn soggy during cooking.

Serves 6

12 *boneless veal cutlets, about 4 ounces each, approximately ¼ inch thick, total weight about 3 pounds*
2 *to 3 teaspoons salt*
½ *to ¾ teaspoon freshly ground pepper*
1 *cup flour, approximately*
3 *eggs, well beaten*

1 *tablespoon cooking oil (optional)*
1½ *to 2 cups fine dry breadcrumbs*
8 *tablespoons butter*
½ *cup lard or cooking oil*
12 *very thick lemon slices, seeds removed*
¼ *cup minced parsley*
capers

Trim any fat and gristle from the cutlets. Make 3 or 4 small vertical cuts around each cutlet so that they will not curl during cooking. Sprinkle with salt and pepper. Have 3 shallow bowls, such as soup plates, ready. Put the flour into the first bowl and the eggs into the second. Stir the tablespoon of cooking oil, if you are using it, into the eggs and blend well (the oil helps the breadcrumbs stick to the beaten eggs). Place the breadcrumbs in the third bowl. Place the bowls in this order (flour, eggs, crumbs) on the kitchen counter as near the stove as possible. Heat the butter and the lard (or cooking oil) in a very large, heavy frying pan over medium heat; there should be about 1 to 1½ inches of fat in the pan. The fat should be very hot and hazy, but not smoking. To test the temperature, drop a bread cube into the fat, which should bubble vigorously around it. Dip the cutlets, one at a time, into the flour and shake off the excess; then dip into beaten egg—do not soak—and shake off the excess; then, dip into the breadcrumbs, coating lightly on all sides and shaking off the excess. Drop cutlets into fat, in one layer; do not crowd them. Cook 3 to 4 minutes on each side, turning over once with tongs or with 2 spoons. Drain immediately on paper towels. Place cooked schnitzels on a heated serving platter and keep warm in a low oven (150 to 175° F.). Place a lemon slice on each and sprinkle the lemon with a little parsley and top with a few capers. Serve hot, or at room temperature, with Rice Pilaff (page 125).

Note: Beware of overheating the lard or oil between batches. Replenish as needed. If it gets too dark, discard it and start with new fat.

Boiled Beef Tongue

The Russian Tea Room kitchens boil tongue in beef or chicken bouillon rather than water for added flavor.

Serves 6 to 8

1 *fresh or smoked beef tongue,*
    weighing 4 to 5 pounds
  beef or chicken bouillon to cover
1 *large onion, studded with 4*
    cloves
1 *celery stalk, with leaves*

½ *lemon, unsliced*
4 *large parsley sprigs*
2 *bay leaves*
1 *tablespoon salt*
6 *peppercorns*

Wash the tongue thoroughly in cold water. Place it in a large kettle, preferably of stainless steel or enamel. Add enough beef or chicken bouillon to cover tongue. Add all the remaining ingredients. Bring to the boiling point and lower heat. Simmer, tightly covered, for about 3 hours and 20 minutes, or until tender. Cool tongue in its broth. Drain tongue. Scrape off vegetables, herbs, etc., and discard. Dry the tongue with paper towels. With a sharp knife, slit skin lengthwise on the underside of the tongue from root to tip and peel off. Cut off the root, small bones and gristle. If tongue is to be served hot, drain broth and return tongue to it to reheat. Slice and, whether hot or cooled, serve with a boiled potato and Horseradish Sauce, (page 135).

Beef en Casserole

Serves 6

2 *pounds boneless beef, chuck or*
    bottom round
2 *teaspoons salt*
½ *teaspoon freshly ground pepper*
3 *tablespoons cooking oil*

1½ *cups chopped onions*
1 *garlic clove, crushed*
1 *cup drained Italian-style*
    tomatoes
1 *cup dry red wine*

Trim all fat from the meat and cut it into 1½-inch cubes. Sprinkle salt and pepper over the meat. Heat the oil in a large heavy saucepan or Dutch oven. Add meat. Over high heat, stirring constantly, brown on all sides for 5 to 8 minutes. Remove meat with a slotted spoon to a heated bowl and keep warm in a low oven (150 to 175°F.). Lower heat under the saucepan to medium, add onions and garlic and cook, stirring constantly for 5 to 8 minutes, or until soft and golden; do not brown. Return meat to saucepan and add tomatoes and wine; mix well. Simmer, covered, over low heat for about 1½ hours, or until meat is tender, stirring frequently. If sauce is too thick, add a little hot water, 1 tablespoon at a time, to achieve desired consistency. If too thin (the water content of tomatoes varies), cook without a cover for the last 15 to 20 minutes. Check seasoning and serve with Rice Pilaff (page 125) and a green salad on the side.

Beef Duchesse with Mushrooms

Serves 6 to 8

1 *rolled beef roast, 3½ to 4*
   pounds (chuck, rump,
   bottom or eye round), at
   room temperature
2 *tablespoons cooking oil*
2 *medium onions, chopped*
1 *large carrot, chopped*
2 *medium tomatoes, peeled and*
   chopped
2 *to 3 teaspoons salt*

½ *teaspoon freshly ground pepper*
½ *cup dry red wine*
2 *tablespoons tomato paste*
2 *bay leaves*
¼ *teaspoon ground ginger*
⅓ *cup minced parsley*
2½ *cups beef bouillon*
2 *tablespoons butter*
½ *pound thinly sliced mushrooms*

Trim any visible fat from the meat. Heat the oil in a large, heavy saucepan or Dutch oven. Add the meat. Over medium heat, brown it on all sides for 10 to 15 minutes. Remove to a platter and keep warm in low oven (150 to 175°F.). Add onions and carrot to saucepan and cook, stirring constantly, for 3 to 5 minutes, or until soft and golden. Return meat to saucepan. Add tomatoes, salt, pepper, wine, tomato paste, bay leaves, ginger, parsley and bouillon. Bring to the boiling point. Turn heat to low. Simmer, covered, for 2½ to 3 hours, or until meat is tender when pierced with a skewer. While beef is cooking, heat butter in a frying pan. Add mushrooms and cook, over medium heat, stirring constantly, for about 3 minutes, or until golden; the mushrooms must still be firm. Transfer cooked meat to a heated plate and keep warm. Skim off all fat from the liquid and vegetables in the saucepan. Purée them in a blender or food processor or strain through a sieve. Return to saucepan and check seasonings. If sauce is too thick, add a little more bouillon, 1 or 2 tablespoons at a time. Add mushrooms and heat through. Slice meat and arrange in overlapping slices on a heated platter. Spoon a little of the sauce over the meat and serve the rest in a sauceboat. Serve with vegetables and Rice Pilaff (page 125).

Stuffed Roast Veal

*A DECORATIVE DISH, WELL WORTH MAKING
FOR A FINE DINNER*

Serves 6

STUFFING

2 tablespoons butter
½ cup minced onion
1 pound lean boneless veal,
      ground
½ large boneless skinned chicken
      breast, ground
2 slices bacon, chopped
2 chicken livers, trimmed
2 slices white bread trimmed of
      crust, soaked in ¼ cup
      heavy cream

2 egg yolks (reserve whites for use
      below)
1 medium garlic clove, chopped
1 tablespoon salt
½ teaspoon freshly ground pepper
1 teaspoon ground thyme or dried
      thyme leaves
2 large carrots of equal size, or 4
      small hard-cooked eggs,
      shelled

VEAL AND SAUCE

1½ to 2 pounds lean boneless veal,
        in 1 (preferably) or 2 slices
1 teaspoon salt
2 egg whites, lightly beaten (see
      above)

6 tablespoons butter
1½ cups chicken consommé
3 tablespoons flour
1 to 1½ cups sour cream

TO MAKE THE STUFFING

Heat the 2 tablespoons butter in a small frying pan. Add the onion.
Cook, stirring constantly, for about 3 minutes or until soft; do not
brown. Turn the onion into a large bowl. Add the ground veal, the
ground chicken, bacon, chicken livers, white bread, egg yolks, garlic,
salt, pepper and thyme. Mix well with a wooden spoon. Put the

mixture through the fine blade of meat grinder 3 times—or process until very fine in a food processor. Reserve.

Trim the carrots to equal length. Drop them into a saucepan with boiling water. Cook over medium heat for about 5 minutes or until almost tender. Drain. The carrots must keep their shape.

Preheat the oven to moderate (350°F.). Pound the meat between 2 sheets of wax paper to the thickness of ¼-inch, forming it into a rectangular shape about 12 by 14 inches. (If using 2 slices of meat, pound them to the same size and thickness. Lay them side by side to form a rectangle. Sew them together with thick kitchen thread, using large overhand stitches.) Place the rectangular slice, with the long side facing you, on a lightly floured working surface. This makes for easier rolling up later. With a sharp knife, make small cuts along the edges of the meat to prevent curling during the cooking. Sprinkle with salt. Spread half the stuffing evenly over the meat, leaving ½ inch of the border uncovered all around. Place the carrots, or the hard-cooked eggs, edge to edge lengthwise in the center of the stuffing. Cover with the remaining stuffing, making sure that carrots (or eggs) are completely covered.

Brush the beaten egg whites along the uncovered border of the meat. Roll up the meat lengthwise to make a roll. Press the ends together to make them stick or the stuffing will ooze out during cooking. Tie the meat roll in 6 or 8 places with kitchen thread.

Heat 4 of the 6 tablespoons of butter in a large, heavy frying pan. Add the meat roll. Brown on all sides over high heat, turning frequently. Transfer the roll to a baking pan that is just large enough to hold it comfortably. Pour the pan juices around the meat. Add 1 cup of the chicken consommé. Bake for 1 to 1¼ hours, basting frequently with the pan juices. If the meat roll begins to look dry, add the remaining ½ cup of chicken consommé.

Turn off the oven when the meat is done. Transfer the roll to a platter and return it to the turned-off oven to keep warm.

TO MAKE THE SAUCE

Remove as much fat as possible from the pan juices. Unless it has already been added, pour the remaining ½ cup of chicken consommé into the pan. Set the pan over medium heat and scrape up all the brown bits at the bottom of the pan. Measure the pan juices—there should be about 1½ cups. If there is a larger amount, cook the pan juices down to 1½ cups. If there is not enough juice, add enough chicken consommé to make 1½ cups.

Heat the remaining 2 tablespoons of butter in a medium-heavy saucepan. Add the flour and cook over medium heat, stirring constantly, for 1 minute. Remove from heat and add the 1½ cups of pan juices. Return to heat and turn to low. Cook, stirring constantly with a wire whisk, until the sauce is smooth and thickened. Remove from heat and beat in 1 cup sour cream for a thick sauce, or 1½ cups for a thinner sauce. Return to low heat and, stirring constantly, heat through, taking care not to boil. Cover and keep warm in the oven.

To serve, remove all threads from the meat. Slice the roll on the bias into 18 slices. Arrange the slices overlapping on a heated platter. Drizzle ⅔ to 1 cup of the sauce over the sliced meat and serve the remaining sauce on the side. Serve with a boiled potato and buttered vegetables.

Veal Kidneys in Madeira or Red Wine

Veal Kidneys in Madeira are traditionally part of the zakuska table, though they make an excellent first or main course. The average weight of a veal kidney is about ½ to ¾ pound. Allow ⅓ to ½ pound of kidneys for each serving.

Serves 6

2½ to 3 pounds veal
    kidneys
5 tablespoons butter
1 tablespoon cooking oil
1½ cups Madeira or dry
    red wine
2 teaspoons salt

¼ teaspoon freshly
    ground pepper
1 to 2 tablespoons fresh
    lemon juice
2 tablespoons minced
    parsley

Remove any fat and membranes from the kidneys. Dry the kidneys with paper towels and cut them into halves lengthwise. With a sharp knife, remove the fat and gristle that runs through the center. Cut the kidneys crosswise into ½-inch slices. Since sliced kidneys send out a certain amount of juice, place them in a strainer for 5 minutes to let them drain. Heat the butter and oil in a large (10- or 12-inch), deep frying pan; do not use an iron pan. While the butter is browning, add the kidneys. Cook over medium-to-high heat, stirring constantly with a wooden spoon, for 2 to 3 minutes on each side or until they are lightly browned on the outside and still pink on the inside. Do not overcook or the kidneys will be tough.

Using a slotted spoon, transfer the kidneys to a heated serving dish and keep them hot in a slow oven (150 to 175°F.). Keep the oven door ajar in order not to overcook the kidneys. Pour the Madeira, or the red wine, into the frying pan. Cook over high heat, scraping up the bits on the bottom of the frying pan, until the wine is boiling. Continue boiling until it has cooked down to half its volume—about ⅔ cup. Turn the heat to very low and add the kidneys to the sauce for 1 minute, stirring with a wooden spoon to coat them with the sauce. Remove from heat and season with salt and pepper. Stir in the lemon juice. Turn into a heated serving dish and sprinkle with the parsley. Serve immediately with hot, cooked rice and a vegetable, such as buttered green beans.

Pilaff of Spring Lamb en Casserole

Fond memories of the Uzbekistan Restaurant in Moscow.

Serves 6

3 pounds boneless lamb
2 tablespoons salad oil
2 tablespoons butter
2 medium onions, thinly sliced
1 can (6 ounces) tomato paste
1 can (1 pound 12 ounces) Italian-
    style plum tomatoes (about
    3½ cups)

1 bay leaf
1½ to 2 teaspoons salt
½ teaspoon freshly ground pepper
½ teaspoon ground coriander
1 to 1½ cups dry red wine

Trim all fat and gristle off the lamb and cut into 1-inch cubes. If any fat and gristle remain after cubing, cut that off too. Combine oil and butter in a large saucepan or Dutch oven. Heat until butter is melted. Add lamb. Cook over high heat, stirring constantly, until meat is browned. Push meat to one side of the saucepan and add the onions. Lower heat to medium and continue to cook, stirring all the time, until onions are tender and golden; do not brown. Add tomato paste, plum tomatoes, bay leaf, salt, pepper, coriander and 1 cup of the wine. Stir until thoroughly blended. Turn heat to low and simmer, covered, for 2¼ to 2½ hours, or until meat is tender. Stir occasionally. If sauce is too thick, add remaining wine, 2 tablespoons at a time. Serve over a bed of hot, cooked rice with a green vegetable.

Chicken Livers en Brochette

An extremely satisfying dish after a great concert.

Serves 6

2 *cups water*
¾ *teaspoon salt*
12 *small (1¼- to 1½-inch) peeled white onions (approximately ¾ pound)*
30 *medium-size chicken livers (approximately 1 pound)*
15 *slices bacon, cut crosswise into halves (approximately ¾ pound)*

½ *teaspoon freshly ground pepper*
3 *medium-ripe but firm tomatoes, cut into quarters (about 1¾ pounds)*
3 *medium green peppers, seeded, membranes removed and cut into quarters*
½ *cup butter, melted*

In a small saucepan, combine the water and ¼ teaspoon of the salt and bring to the boiling point. Add the onions. Cook over low heat, uncovered for 5 to 7 minutes or until barely tender and still firm. Drain and set aside. Wipe the chicken livers with paper towels, and remove any fat and connective tissue. Put them into a bowl and toss with the remaining ½ teaspoon salt and ¼ teaspoon of the pepper. Wrap each liver in ½ slice of bacon. On each of six 12-inch skewers thread 1 chicken liver, 1 tomato quarter, 1 chicken liver, 1 pepper quarter, 1 chicken liver, 1 tomato quarter, 1 chicken liver, 1 pepper quarter and 1 chicken liver.

Arrange skewers on a large broiling rack. Brush each with some of the melted butter. Broil 4 to 6 inches from heat source for 5 to 10 minutes, or until the bacon is golden brown and the vegetables tender. Turn frequently and brush frequently with melted butter. To serve, slide chicken livers and vegetables from skewers and season with more salt and pepper to taste. Serve over a bed of hot, boiled rice with lightly cooked sweet-pepper strips.

Vegetarian Casserole

Believe it or not, people rave about the fact that vegetarian meals are served at The Russian Tea Room. This really appeals to strong-minded vegetarians. So—here is another example of the wide diversity of The Russian Tea Room menu.

Serves 6

1 *eggplant, weighing approximately ¾ to 1 pound*
2 *medium zucchini, weighing approximately ¾ to 1 pound*
2 *tablespoons salt*
4 *tablespoons olive oil*
2 *large onions, chopped*
1 *large carrot, grated*
3 *cups canned Italian-style tomatoes*
2 *tablespoons minced parsley*
2 *tablespoons minced dill weed*
2 *garlic cloves, minced*
1 *tablespoon Worcestershire sauce salt*

freshly ground pepper
1 *cup fresh green beans trimmed and broken into pieces or frenched, or one 10-ounce package frozen frenched beans*
2 *cups cooked kidney beans or cooked large white lima beans, or one 15-ounce can kidney beans*
2 *tablespoons fresh white breadcrumbs*
3 *tablespoons freshly grated Parmesan cheese*
2 *tablespoons butter, cut into small pieces*
sour cream

Preheat oven to low (325°F). Cut any bruises off the skins of the eggplant and the zucchini. Cut them into ⅓-inch slices. Place the eggplant slices in a colander in 3 layers and sprinkle each layer with about 1 tablespoon of the salt. Place the zucchini slices in another colander in 3 layers and sprinkle each layer with the remaining salt. Set colanders in the sink or a deep platter to allow the salted vegetables to drain. Let stand at room temperature for 1 to 2 hours. After draining, use your hands to squeeze out as much liquid as possible from both the eggplant and zucchini. In a large frying pan, heat the oil. Add the onions and cook, stirring constantly, for 3 to 5 minutes, or until soft; do not brown. Add the grated carrot and the tomatoes. Cook over low-to-medium heat, stirring frequently, until the sauce is thick and soft. Add parsley, dill, garlic and Worcestershire sauce and cook for 2 more minutes. Season to taste; be careful about adding salt, as the eggplant and the zucchini will be salty from their earlier treatment. In a buttered 2-quart baking dish or casserole, make alternate layers of the tomato sauce and all the other vegetables, beginning and ending with the tomato sauce. Combine breadcrumbs and cheese and sprinkle on the top of the tomato sauce. Dot with butter. Bake for about 1 hour, or until the top is golden and bubbly. Serve hot, with a bowl of sour cream on the side.

Broiled Mushrooms on Toast

A salute to the Savoy Grill in London. Choose clean, white, plump mushrooms of even size that are closed on the underside, hiding the gills. Visible brown gills are signs that the mushrooms are not fresh.

Serves 4

1 *pound medium-size mushrooms*
1 *cup melted butter*
1 *teaspoon salt*

⅛ *teaspoon freshly ground pepper*
4 *to 8 hot white toast slices,*
   buttered, crusts removed

Wipe the mushrooms clean with paper towels, or swirl them quickly in a bowl of cold water, drain and dry each mushroom carefully with paper towels. The mushrooms must be absolutely dry. Put the mushrooms in a bowl and pour the melted butter over them. Toss with your hands or two spoons until each mushroom is well coated with butter. Lightly oil the broiler rack with a piece of paper towel dipped in cooking oil. Place the mushrooms on the rack, cup side down. Using a pastry brush, brush the mushrooms with the remaining butter in the bowl. Broil in a preheated broiler 5 inches from the source of the heat until golden. Using tongs, turn the caps and brush again with butter. Broil 3 more minutes. Make toast and butter it while mushrooms are broiling. Divide mushrooms evenly on toast slices, salt and pepper, and serve immediately.

SALADS
& COLD PLATTERS

Over the years, our Salad Platters have become year-round favorites. Our guests like the variety, the generous portions and the presentation. Many of our salads are served on a bed of salad greens, with potato salad and cole slaw, lemon wedges, pickle slices and sliced hard-boiled eggs, and we pretty them up with radish roses, carrot curls, scallion fans, cherry tomatoes, olives and pimiento. The dressing is served separately and each guest has his or her choice.

The Salad Platters of
The Russian Tea Room

Here are some of our Salad Platter combinations:

Tongue, Turkey and Smoked Salmon Slices
Half a Cold Roast Duckling
Salami and Smoked Tongue Slices
Sliced Cold Cotelettes
Tuna Salad
Chicken Salad
Whole Shrimps
Imported Smoked Salmon slices with Chopped Onion, Capers,
    Lemon Wedges and Buttered Black Bread
Nova Scotia Salmon Slices with Onion Rings, Capers and Lemon
    Wedges
Chef's Salad
Fruit Salad with Cottage Cheese
Cottage Cheese with Sour Cream, with Tomato and Parsley
Ogurtze

Chef's Salad

Our chef's salad, served "regular," "chopped," "medium chopped" or "birdseed," according to the special whims of our guests, is a favorite at lunch for many film people. Helen Gurley Brown, editor-in-chief of Cosmopolitan *magazine, lives on this dish—"birdseed" style.*

Serves 1

2 cups mixed salad greens (preferably equal amounts of escarole, romaine and iceberg lettuce) in bite-size pieces

⅓ cup julienne strips cooked smoked tongue

⅓ cup julienne strips cooked white turkey meat

⅓ cup julienne strips boiled ham

¼ cup julienne strips Swiss cheese

1 hard-cooked egg, cut into quarters

4 cherry tomatoes or 4 tomato slices

1 or 2 carrot curls

4 parsley sprigs

1 black olive

1 teaspoon minced pimiento dressing to taste

Line a good-sized individual salad bowl with the salad greens. Group tongue, turkey, ham and cheese in a spokelike fashion on the greens. Arrange the egg quarters, tomatoes, carrot curls and parsley around the meats. Top the center with the olive. Sprinkle ¼ teaspoon minced pimiento on each egg quarter. Serve with any favored dressing on the side.

Chicken Salad

Serves 6

⅓ cup salad oil
2 to 3 tablespoons white vinegar
  or fresh lemon juice
¼ teaspoon salt
⅛ teaspoon freshly ground pepper
2 to 3 drops Tabasco, or to taste
½ to 1 teaspoon A 1 Sauce
  (optional)
4 cups cubed cooked chicken
  (preferably white meat
  only)

1 cup thinly sliced celery, white
  part only
¾ to 1 cup mayonnaise
  salad greens
⅓ cup thinly sliced scallions, white
  and green parts
  cole slaw (⅓ cup, or to taste per
  serving)
1 cherry tomato per serving
½ dill pickle per serving

Combine the salad oil, vinegar or lemon juice, salt, pepper, Tabasco and the A 1 Sauce, if you are using it. Mix thoroughly. Put the diced chicken in a bowl (do not use aluminum) and toss with this dressing, making sure that all the chicken pieces are coated with it. Cover and refrigerate for 2 to 3 hours, stirring once or twice. At serving time, combine marinated chicken with the celery and the mayonnaise. Pile in one heap on a large platter, or in 6 separate servings, over salad greens. Sprinkle with the scallions. Garnish with cole slaw, cherry tomatoes and dill pickles.

Note: Adding the mayonnaise and celery at serving time to the marinated chicken makes for a crisper salad.

VARIATIONS

Instead of scallions, sprinkle with ⅓ cup drained capers.

Instead of scallions, top with ⅔ cup of sliced pimiento-stuffed olives.

Salade Olivier

*A GLORIFIED CHICKEN SALAD AND A TANGY RUSSIAN
ALTERNATE TO PLAIN CHICKEN SALAD THAT TAKES ITS NAME
FROM ONE OF TSAR NICHOLAS II'S CHEFS*

Serves 12 as zakuska

Serves 6 as main dish

4 *to 5 cups water*
1 *medium onion, chopped*
1 *medium carrot, chopped*
1 *celery stalk with leaves, chopped*
1 *leek, white and green parts,
    chopped (optional)*
1 *bay leaf*

1 *teaspoon salt*
½ *teaspoon freshly ground pepper*
¼ *teaspoon dried thyme*
2 *whole chicken breasts, each
    weighing approximately 1
    pound*

To prepare chicken, combine the water and all the ingredients
(except the chicken breasts) in a saucepan. Bring to the boiling point,
lower the heat and simmer, covered, for 10 to 15 minutes. In the
meantime, remove the excess fat from the chicken breasts. Add them to
the broth, bring to the boiling point and lower the heat. Simmer,
covered, for 20 minutes. Cool breasts, preferably in the broth. Carefully
remove all skin, bones and gristle. Cut into neat ½- to ¾-inch pieces.
There should be 3 to 4 cups of chicken. Place on a dish, cover with
plastic wrap and refrigerate if the salad is to be served hours later.

3 *medium potatoes (about 1
    pound), freshly cooked but
    still firm*
4 *hard-cooked eggs*
½ *pound cooked ham, in one piece*
1 *small cucumber*

2 *medium-size firm, sweet apples*
2 *tablespoons fresh lemon juice*
3 *to 4 cups chicken pieces*
2 *small to medium tomatoes, cut
    into 6 slices*

It is essential that all the ingredients for Salade Olivier be at room
temperature when the salad is being assembled; if any of the ingre-

dients have been refrigerated, bring them back to room temperature before combining. Keep all the ingredients in covered bowls until assembly time. Peel the potatoes and cut into ½-inch cubes. Coarsely chop 2 of the hard-cooked eggs and thinly slice the remaining; set sliced eggs aside. Cut the ham into ½-inch pieces. Peel the cucumber and cut into quarters. Scoop out the seeds and cut the cucumber quarters into ½-inch pieces. Peel the apples, core them and cut them into ¼-inch pieces. Sprinkle the apple pieces with the lemon juice, coating them on all sides; this will prevent them from darkening. Combine the potatoes, chopped eggs, ham, cucumber, apple and chicken pieces in a bowl. Keep in a cool place, but do not chill, while you make the dressing.

DRESSING

1 *cup mayonnaise, preferably homemade*	1 *to 2 tablespoons drained capers (if large, chop)*
⅔ *cup sour cream*	*salt*
2 *teaspoons Dijon mustard*	*freshly ground pepper*
⅓ *cup dill pickles cut into small cubes*	2 *tablespoons minced dill weed or parsley*

For the dressing, combine mayonnaise, sour cream, mustard, dill pickles and capers and mix thoroughly. Taste for seasoning and add salt and pepper to taste. Toss the salad with the dressing, taking care not to break or crush the pieces of the various ingredients. Pile the salad into a platter or a salad bowl. Decorate with tomato and egg slices. Sprinkle dill or parsley over all and serve immediately.

Ogurtze Salad

Ogurtze *means cucumber in Russian. This salad is delightful for a summer-evening supper or as a side dish with hearty fare like shashlik. The mixing of yogurt with sour cream for dressing gives a lighter taste, closer to the Russian sour cream than ours. On visits to Russia we have sometimes subsisted on vodka, caviar and Ogurtze Salad—not too bad!*

Serves 1

1 *small or ½ large cucumber, peeled and sliced*
6 *large red radishes, trimmed, washed and sliced*
1 *cup plain yogurt*

⅓ *cup sour cream*
¼ *teaspoon salt (optional)*
2 *to 3 medium scallions with unblemished green tops, trimmed and washed*

Assemble in an individual salad or glass bowl. Place the cucumber slices in a circle around the top edge of the bowl. Place radishes, reserving 5 slices, also in a circle, below the cucumber slices. Combine yogurt and sour cream in a bowl and beat with a wire whisk until light and well mixed. Beat in salt, if you are using it. Place the mixture in the center of the bowl. Top with the reserved radish slices, standing them up in a circle. Cut the green tops of the scallions into thin rounds; save the white part for another use. Sprinkle scallion rounds over the salad. Serve immediately.

Cucumber Salad

Cucumbers have a special place in Russian cuisine. They are among the few fresh vegetables readily available in Russia and their taste goes very well with cotelettes and shashliks.

Serves 4 to 6

3 medium-to-large cucumbers
2 teaspoons salt
4 to 5 tablespoons sour cream
2 tablespoons lemon juice

⅓ teaspoon sugar, or to taste
¼ teaspoon freshly ground white
    pepper

Peel the cucumbers, preferably with a vegetable peeler. With a sharp knife, cut cucumbers into paper-thin slices—or use a slicer or the thin-slicing disk of the food processor. Layer the cucumbers in a shallow dish, sprinkling a little of the salt between layers. Let cucumbers stand at cool room temperature for 1 to 2 hours. Drain off the juice and, using your hands, squeeze the cucumbers as dry as possible. Beat together sour cream, lemon juice, sugar and pepper. Add the cucumbers and toss. Check the seasoning. Cover with plastic wrap and chill before serving.

Potato Salad

Along with bread and soup, potatoes are the Russians' staple diet. They dress them up any way they can for variety. Here's a happy summer choice.

Serves 6

6 to 8 medium potatoes (about 2
    to 3 pounds depending on
    size)
⅔ cup mayonnaise
⅔ cup sour cream
1 tablespoon minced onion
1 tablespoon white vinegar or to
    taste

1 tablespoon fresh lemon juice
1 teaspoon Dijon mustard
  salt
¼ teaspoon freshly ground pepper
⅓ cup minced pimiento
2 tablespoons minced parsley
  salad greens

Boil the potatoes until just tender when pierced with the point of a knife. Drain, and as soon as sufficiently cool to handle, peel and cut into small dice. Turn the potatoes into a deep bowl. While potatoes are cooking, make the dressing. Combine mayonnaise and sour cream in a bowl and beat with a wire whisk until well mixed. Add onion, vinegar, lemon juice and mustard and blend thoroughly. Add salt, but taste as you are adding it; the mayonnaise and mustard may be salty already. Add pepper and pimiento and mix again. Spoon over the potatoes and toss with a fork to coat them evenly. Cover the bowl and chill until serving time. Sprinkle with parsley and serve on salad greens.

Cole Slaw

Serves 6 to 12

4 cups (about 1 pound) finely
    shredded green cabbage
⅔ cup finely shredded carrots
½ cup diced green pepper
⅓ cup minced onion

Dressing (see below)
2 tablespoons minced pimiento
   salad greens
2 tablespoons minced parsley

Combine cabbage, carrots, green pepper and onion in a bowl. Mix well. Add dressing and pimiento. Toss to mix. Line a salad bowl with salad greens. Pile slaw on salad greens and sprinkle with parsley. Or use to accompany individual salads (tuna, chicken, potato, etc.)—about ½ cup Cole Slaw for each serving.

DRESSING

Makes about 1⅓ cups

⅔ cup mayonnaise
⅔ cup sour cream
1 tablespoon white vinegar
1 tablespoon fresh lemon juice
1 teaspoon drained prepared
   horseradish, or to taste

2 to 3 teaspoons sugar, or to taste
½ teaspoon salt
¼ teaspoon freshly ground pepper

Combine mayonnaise and sour cream in a bowl. Beat with a wire whisk until blended and fluffy. Add the remaining ingredients and beat again to mix thoroughly. Taste for seasoning; you may want a tarter or a sweeter dressing.

Dressings

Russian Dressing

Many of our guests prefer Russian Dressing to any other on sandwiches, shrimp cocktails, chef's salads. They probably feel it's de rigueur at The Russian Tea Room—and for good reason.

Makes about 3⅓ cups

1½ cups mayonnaise
½ cup sour cream
⅔ cup chili sauce
1 tablespoon fresh lemon juice
2 tablespoons minced dill pickle
1 tablespoon minced green pepper
2 tablespoons minced onion
4 teaspoons finely grated fresh
        horseradish or drained
        bottled horseradish

2 teaspoons Worcestershire sauce
¼ teaspoon Tabasco
2 teaspoons sugar
½ teaspoon salt
⅛ teaspoon freshly ground pepper
½ teaspoon paprika
1 tablespoon minced parsley

Combine all ingredients in a food processor or blender. Blend until thoroughly mixed, but do not overblend. Refrigerate in a covered jar until serving time. Stir before using.

Italian Dressing

When Italian architects built St. Petersburg they introduced Italian food at the same time. For instance, we are told that the best (and only) pasta in Russia is still to be had in Leningrad.

Makes about 3 cups

2 cups salad or olive oil
2 tablespoons red wine vinegar
¼ cup lemon juice
2 tablespoons spicy brown
    mustard
1 teaspoon sugar
1 teaspoon salt

¼ teaspoon freshly ground pepper
1 garlic clove, minced
2 tablespoons minced onion
2 tablespoons minced parsley
1 tablespoon minced fresh
    tarragon leaves or 1
    teaspoon dried tarragon

Combine all the ingredients in a food processor or blender. Blend until thoroughly mixed. Store in a covered jar until serving time. Shake well before using.

French Dressing

Most "house" dressings are French dressing; but, understandably, ours is Russian. Still, chacun à son goût!

Makes about 3 cups

2½ cups salad oil
¼ cup white vinegar
3 tablespoons chili sauce
1 tablespoon fresh lemon juice
1 tablespoon paprika
1 teaspoon minced onion
½ small garlic clove, minced

1 teaspoon sugar
¼ teaspoon salt
⅛ teaspoon freshly ground white
    pepper
¼ teaspoon Tabasco sauce
2 egg yolks

Combine all ingredients except the egg yolks in a food processor or blender. Turn on and off a few times—enough to blend thoroughly. Add the egg yolks. Process for a few seconds or until blended. Do not overprocess or mixture will emulsify. Store in a covered jar until serving time. Shake well before using.

Roquefort Dressing

Makes about 3½ cups

1½ cups mayonnaise
½ cup sour cream
¼ cup salad oil
 2 tablespoons vinegar
 1 tablespoon fresh lemon juice
 1 teaspoon minced shallot (about
        ½ small shallot)
 2 teaspoons Worcestershire sauce

½ small garlic clove, minced
⅛ teaspoon salt (none if Roquefort
        is very salty)
¼ teaspoon white pepper
¼ teaspoon Tabasco
 6 ounces Roquefort cheese,
        crumbled
⅓ cup minced parsley

Combine all ingredients except the cheese and parsley in a food processor or blender. Process for a few seconds, or until just blended. Add cheese and parsley and turn motor on and off quickly 3 or 4 times, only until cheese and parsley are incorporated in the dressing. Refrigerate in a covered jar until serving time. Stir before using.

SANDWICHES
& OMELETS

The long association of The Russian Tea Room with Carnegie Hall helped to create a mini-menu of sandwiches for musicians on a break or late-night patrons after the concert. Russian Tea Room sandwiches are substantial affairs and very much in demand at lunch, supper and after-theater time, when people are not up to a whole meal but still want something good to eat. With the exception of the classic bacon, lettuce and tomato and the club sandwich, we serve open-faced sandwiches with a great variety of toppings.

Sandwiches

Here are some favorites that you might like to re-create at home and serve in The Russian Tea Room manner.

Smoked Salmon and Bermuda Onion
Smoked Salmon and Cream Cheese
Red Caviar and Sliced Eggs
Boneless Sardines with Lemon Wedges
Sliced Breast of Turkey
Imported Ham
Imported Salami
Swiss Cheese
American Cheese
Chopped Chicken Liver
Chicken Salad
Tunafish Salad
Egg Salad
Roast Turkey, Smoked Tongue and Imported Swiss Cheese
Smoked Ham and Imported Swiss Cheese
Roast Turkey and Chopped Chicken Liver
Smoked Ham and Turkey

We use our traditional black Russian bread, though a guest may have any other kind of bread he or she fancies. For a single sandwich, a large slice of black bread is cut in two diagonally and topped with, and surrounded by, a generous portion of the food it calls for. The sandwiches are garnished appropriately—red caviar comes with sliced eggs, smoked salmon with thinly sliced Bermuda onion rings, to give two examples. The sandwich plate also holds a good helping of freshly made cole slaw nestling on a bed of salad greens, sliced or cherry tomatoes, sliced pickles, green or Polish dill, black or green olives, radish roses and a slice of carrot curling around a scallion. The dressing is the guests' choice. The bread may be buttered if requested.

Omelets

Along with sandwiches, omelets are in great demand at The RTR by guests who want a light meal. Favorites are the Red Caviar Omelet with Sour Cream, the Mushroom Omelet and the Smoked Salmon Omelet, for which recipes follow. We serve our omelets with no garnish other than parsley, and with a boiled potato or vegetable if desired. Each omelet is made to order, one at a time, from 3 eggs.

Here are a few tips for omelet making. Omelets must be made quickly and the whole operation should ideally take no more time than 1 minute. Therefore, if the omelet is to be filled, have the filling ready. Do not overbeat eggs; 20 seconds should do it. Use water (1 teaspoon cold water for each egg) for a light omelet; never milk or cream, which would toughen it. Use a proper omelet pan; this is essential. The pan should be 8 to 10 inches in diameter, well seasoned to inhibit sticking, with rounded, sloping shoulders to shape the omelet nicely and allow it to slide out easily. Ideally the pan should be of medium weight and made of cast aluminum, tin-lined copper, enameled cast iron or Teflon-lined aluminum. Use sweet butter only, and not more than specified in the recipes since too much butter will make a wrinkled omelet. After use, wipe out your omelet pan with paper toweling, but do not wash. If something burns on the bottom, scour the pan with salt and fine steel wool—not soap-filled pads. Rinse, dry and reseason pan if necessary. To season, half fill the pan with cooking oil, set over lowest heat and let stand without a cover for 1 hour. Turn off heat and let oil cool in the pan. Pour out and save for cooking if you desire. Wipe the pan with paper toweling. Make only 1 omelet at a time and serve immediately on a warm, not hot, plate.

Remember, a perfect omelet requires practice.

Red Caviar Omelet with Sour Cream

Fit for the Czars—sour cream is spooned over the omelet after serving.

Serves 1

3 eggs, at room temperature
½ teaspoon salt
¼ teaspoon freshly ground pepper
1 tablespoon water
1 tablespoon sweet butter

2 ounces red caviar
    (approximately 1 heaped
    tablespoon)
1 tablespoon sour cream
    parsley for garnish

With the flat side of a fork, beat the eggs with salt and pepper 20 seconds, or only until well mixed; do not overbeat. Beat in water to lighten omelet. Place butter in an 8- to 10-inch omelet pan over medium-to-high heat and heat until bubbly. When the butter no longer foams, pour in eggs; they should sizzle. Let the eggs set for 5 or 6 seconds. With the flat side of a fork in one hand, stir the eggs in a circular motion. At the same time, with the other hand, tilt and shake the pan gently back and forth in a continuous movement so that uncooked egg portions flow underneath. Continue until omelet is barely set and the top creamy and moist. Remove pan from heat, loosen omelet edges with fork where necessary, and shake pan gently to loosen omelet. Spoon red caviar onto omelet. Fold omelet in half and slide onto a warm, not hot, plate. Spoon sour cream in the center of the top of the omelet. Garnish with parsley and serve immediately, with a boiled potato if desired. Accompany with ½ cup sour cream separately in a little bowl.

Mushroom Omelet

Mushrooms sautéed in butter are folded into the omelet.

Serves 1

3 *eggs, at room temperature*
½ *teaspoon salt*
¼ *teaspoon freshly ground pepper*
1 *tablespoon water*

1 *tablespoon sweet butter*
½ *cup thinly sliced mushrooms
sautéed in butter (see
below)*

With the flat side of a fork, beat the eggs with salt and pepper 20 seconds or only until well mixed; do not overbeat. Beat in water to lighten omelet. Place butter in an 8- to 10-inch omelet pan over medium-to-high heat and heat until bubbly. When the butter no longer foams, pour in eggs; they should sizzle. Let the eggs set for 5 or 6 seconds. With the flat side of a fork in one hand, stir the eggs in a circular motion. At the same time, with the other hand, tilt and shake the pan gently back and forth in a continuous movement so that uncooked egg portions flow underneath. Continue until omelet is barely set and the top creamy and moist. Remove pan from heat, loosen omelet edges with fork where necessary, and shake pan gently to loosen omelet. Arrange mushrooms in a line in the center of omelet. Fold omelet in half, enclosing mushrooms, and slide onto a warm, not hot, plate. Garnish with parsley and serve immediately, with a boiled potato if desired.

To sauté mushrooms: Heat 1 tablespoon butter in a small frying pan. Add ½ cup thinly sliced mushrooms. Cook over moderate heat, stirring constantly, for 3 to 5 minutes or until golden. Remove from heat; use to fill omelet.

❀❀❀❀❀❀❀

Smoked Salmon Omelet

Serves 1

Proceed as for Mushroom Omelet, but instead of mushrooms sautéed in butter, fill the omelet with ½ cup finely chopped smoked salmon at room temperature.

DESSERTS
-
TEA & COFFEE

Pour la bonne bouche *is a French saying that describes the closing food or drink of a meal—the one that gives it a lovely, lingering last taste.* Pour la bonne bouche *is how we describe the finishing touches of our dinners—The Russian Tea Room desserts, teas and coffees. As our guests tell us, our desserts are our crowning glory. Over and again, strong-minded men and women who say No to dessert on principle will yield to the lure of our delicious Russian and American sweet endings to their meals. As you will see from the following pages, the choice is great and the range wide, from exotic Baklava through Russian Cream to tangy Cranberry Kissel, and to the luscious Marzipan Potatoes that bring back childhood memories to those who grew up in Europe.*

But if you are really not in the mood for dessert, you may want to end your meal simply with our special tea, served in one of a variety of ways, or one of our coffees, American or espresso.

Paska and Kulich

Kulich is a tall, cylindrical yeast cake-bread (like a tea cake) with a mushroom cap of white icing and Paska is a sweet cheesecake shaped like a pyramid with a flattened top, made of pot cheese, eggs, cream, butter and glazed fruit. They are essential parts of the Russian Easter table.

At The Russian Tea Room we serve them both at our own Easter and at the Russian Easter, which might fall on the same day—or the two might come as far apart as 6 weeks. At this time you may also admire our two front windows in the restaurant, decorated especially for the most important holiday in the Russian calendar. Gene Moore, the wonderful artist who designs the windows at Tiffany's down the street, also designs our windows, and he goes wild at Easter—sometimes there are dozens of real eggs suspended on ribbons and blowing and swaying in a pattern created by an electric fan. Or a Russian Easter table is set with Paska, Kulich, a samovar and special painted Russian eggs. Russian women design the eggs, called pysanki, at home and we display them—painted on wood or marble, real eggs, paper eggs, little dolls and animals and mushroom houses that open to reveal tiny toys inside.

Besides being delicious, Kulich and Paska are symbolic foods. Pashka is believed to have come to Russia from Byzantium. In the old days, Russia's faithful observed a very strict Lenten fast that excluded all meat and dairy products; and all other foods were eaten sparingly. But when the long winter finally blossomed into spring at Easter, people feasted once more. The Kulich represented the cakes and breads that the faithful had abstained from during Lent, and the Paska stood for the dairy foods that were not allowed during that time. The cakes were taken to be blessed by the priest before the midnight Easter ceremony.

In honor of the great feast of Easter, both Kulich and Paska were decorated—with pastry flowers and with the initials XB, which stand for "Christos Voskress," "Christ is Risen" in Russian. Paska and Kulich are served as dessert throughout the Easter season at The Russian Tea Room. They are always served together, a scoop of Paska placed on a slice of Kulich, as a glorious Russian Tea Room Easter dessert that you can duplicate at home.

Paska

Since Paska must be very dry and very smooth, it is better to use farmer's cheese than the traditional pot cheese, which is not as dry and smooth as the former. Our own cottage cheese does not serve for Paska because it contains too much moisture and has not enough body. Since farmer's cheese and even pot cheese are very dry, do not try to force them through a sieve. The only way to get a truly smooth and dry Paska is to beat the mixture long and hard. Needless to say, the effort is very worthwhile because a good Paska is a truly glorious dessert. A warning: do not use a blender or food processor to blend the Paska as it will only plasticize it. A true Russian Paska is molded in the shape of a pyramid. The mold consists of 4 wooden boards that notch together. Since these molds are rare, an ordinary flowerpot will serve the purpose, provided it is used as explained in the recipe below. Also explained is the way to decorate the Paska in the traditional Russian manner.

Serves 10 to 12

2½ pounds farmer's cheese or pot cheese
1 cup butter, very soft but not melted
1 cup heavy cream
2 large eggs or 2 medium eggs
1½ cups superfine sugar
1½ teaspoons vanilla

1 cup mixed diced glazed fruit
1 cup golden raisins, plumped in hot water and drained
½ cup chopped blanched almonds glazed fruit, golden raisins for decorating
1 to 2 tablespoons brandy, rum or rosewater

Have all the ingredients at room temperature. In a large bowl, break up the farmer's cheese into small pieces; do not use a food processor. Add alternate small amounts of butter and heavy cream to the cheese, and beat with a wooden spoon until very soft and smooth. Beat for at least 10 minutes—the longer the beating, the smoother the mixture—and smoothness is essential. It is easier to beat by hand because an electric mixer or beater gets clogged with the thick mixture. In another bowl, beat together the eggs and sugar until very thick and light. Beat egg mixture into cheese gradually, and beat until very well blended and smooth. Beat in the vanilla. Reserve ¼ cup glazed fruit and ¼ cup raisins for later decoration. Beat remaining glazed fruits, raisins and almonds, and the brandy, rum or rosewater, into the mixture and beat until well mixed. Wash and dry a 7-inch new clay flowerpot. Line it as smoothly as possible with several layers of clean cheesecloth, letting about 4 or 5 inches of cheesecloth hang over the rim of the pot on each side. Carefully spoon the Paska into the pot and press it down into a solid mass. Fold the cheesecloth over the Paska. Top with a plate smaller than the top of the flowerpot. Put a weight (cans, brick, etc.) on the plate. Set the flowerpot on a rack on another plate. Let the Paska drain at room temperature for 1 to 2 hours. Pour off any accumulated liquid and set plate, rack and flowerpot in the refrigerator. Refrigerate for at least 24 hours and let drain completely; the Paska must be dry. To serve, unwrap the cheesecloth that covers it. Hold a serving plate over the flowerpot and flip it upside down to unmold. Carefully peel off the cheesecloth. Decorate the Paska with a row of raisins circling the rim of the top and with 4 rows of glazed fruit and raisins running from top to bottom on 4 sides. With raisins, outline the letters XB on one side to indicate, in the Cyrillic alphabet, "Christos Voskress." Top the Paska with a paper rose. Cut into slices to serve.

Note: Paska is an excellent sweet for buffets, but it should be accompanied by Kulich as a contrast (or some other dry, not overly sweet cake such as sponge).

Kulich

This is a fruit-filled cake-bread with a mushroom-shaped top, resembling an Italian panettone. When thoroughly cooled Kilich may be frozen.

Makes 2 cakes

DOUGH

½ cup lukewarm water (105 to 115°F.)
2 envelopes active dry yeast
2 teaspoons salt
½ cup sugar
1½ cups lukewarm milk (105 to 115°F.)
1 cup butter, melted and cooled

4 egg yolks
4 eggs
8 cups sifted flour
½ cup chopped blanched almonds
1½ cups golden raisins
½ cup diced mixed glazed fruit
grated rind of 1 lemon

Pour the water into a large bowl and sprinkle the yeast over it. Stir to dissolve yeast. Stir in salt, sugar, milk, butter, egg yolks and eggs, almonds, raisins, glazed fruit and lemon rind. Beat vigorously until well mixed. Beat in flour gradually; then beat 10 minutes by hand or 3 minutes with an electric beater at medium speed. The batter will be smooth and shiny. Cover the bowl with a damp kitchen towel and let it rise in a warm, draft-free place until doubled in bulk, or for about 1 hour. While the dough is rising, generously butter and flour two 2-pound coffee cans. Shake out excess flour. Beat the risen dough for 2 minutes and divide it into 2 equal amounts. Turn the dough into the coffee cans. The cans will be about half full. Cover both cans again with a damp kitchen towel and let the dough rise in a warm, draft-free place until doubled in bulk—this should take about 35 or 40 minutes. The dough will reach the top of each can. While the dough is rising again, preheat the oven to low-moderate (325°F.). Remove the towel covering the dough. Bake for 1 hour or until cakes test clean and are puffed, browned and firm to the touch. If the tops brown too quickly, moisten a paper towel and cover the tops to prevent burning. Place cakes, still in cans, on cake racks and cool to lukewarm. Then invert carefully on racks to cool completely. Stand cakes upright on serving platters. Mushroom top will be baked firm and will not squash.

FROSTING

2 *cups sifted confectioner's sugar*   *colored sprinkles*
3 *tablespoons lemon juice*

In a small bowl, beat together confectioner's sugar and lemon juice until smooth. Spread equal amounts of the frosting over the top of the 2 cakes, allowing the excess to drip down the sides. Sprinkle frosting immediately with sprinkles.

To serve the Kulich: Slice off the mushroom-shaped cap. Cut round slices from the cake and cut these into halves. Replace cap to keep the kulich from drying out.

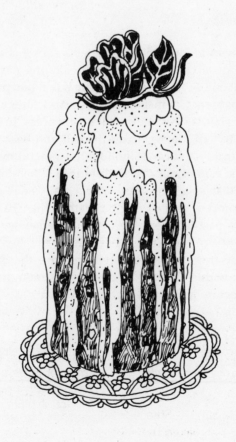

Lodichka

A BUTTER-CREAM-FILLED, CHOCOLATE-COVERED MACAROON SHAPED LIKE A SMALL CHOCOLATE BOAT

This is a great favorite with conductor Daniel Barenboim and many others. He told me it was his first dessert experience as a child at The Russian Tea Room, and it remains his favorite now.

Makes 12 pastries

PASTRY

½ cup almond paste
½ cup sugar
1 tablespoon cornstarch

2 egg whites, at room temperature
⅛ teaspoon salt

Preheat the oven to low (250°F.). Butter a cookie sheet and coat it with flour; shake off excess flour. Place the almond paste, sugar and cornstarch into a bowl. As if you were making pie pastry, cut the mixture to the consistency of meal, using a pastry cutter or 2 knives. Or process quickly in food processor; do not overprocess. In another bowl, beat the egg whites until foamy. Add the salt and beat until stiff and shiny. Working quickly and carefully, fold the almond mixture into the beaten egg whites. Spoon out the mixture into 3-inch-long ovals onto the cookie sheet. Or use a pastry bag with a plain small tube. Bake for 1½ hours. (The process is a drying-out rather than baking.) Do not remove the baked pastries from the oven immediately, but open the door and let them cool for 5 minutes in the oven. Remove and cool them further away from drafts. Carefully remove the cooled pastries from cookie sheet with a spatula. (Pastries will stiffen during cooling.) Cool completely before topping with Butter Cream.

BUTTER CREAM

1¼ cups butter, at room
        temperature and very soft
1 egg white
⅛ teaspoon salt
⅔ cup superfine sugar

½ teaspoon instant coffee
1 teaspoon warm water
1 tablespoon brandy or creme de
        cacao (optional)

In a small bowl, cream the butter with a wooden spoon to the consistency of mayonnaise. In a larger bowl, beat the egg white until foamy. Beat in the salt. Gradually beat in the sugar, 2 tablespoons at a time, beating until stiff but not dry. Add the creamed butter, 1 tablespoon at a time, to the beaten egg white and beat after each addition. Dissolve the instant coffee in the water and beat it into the butter mixture. Beat in the brandy or creme de cacao, if you are using it, and blend thoroughly. Cover the bowl with plastic wrap and refrigerate until stiff. While the Butter Cream is chilling, make the Chocolate Glaze.

CHOCOLATE GLAZE

1½ *squares (1½ ounces)*   2 *tablespoons white corn syrup*
    unsweetened chocolate,   1½ *cups sifted confectioner's sugar*
    chopped   1 *tablespoon finely chopped*
3 *tablespoons water*   *pistachio nuts*

Combine the chocolate, water and corn syrup in the top of a double boiler. Cook over hot, not boiling water or over low heat, stirring constantly, until chocolate has melted and mixture is smooth. Beat in sugar gradually until very smooth. Remove from heat and cool thoroughly.

TO ASSEMBLE LODICHKA

Place the pastries on a large platter. With a knife dipped in cold water, spread the butter cream in the shape of a boat keel on each pastry. (Dip the knife in cold water from time to time as necessary.) Smooth the Butter Cream on all sides. Chill until firm. With a pastry brush, brush Chocolate Glaze over the Butter Cream on each pastry. Or dip each pastry, butter-cream side down, into the Chocolate Glaze. Sprinkle about ¼ teaspoon chopped pistachio nuts on the middle of the top of each Lodichka. Refrigerate until serving time.

Charlottka (Charlotte Russe)

A MOLDED CAKE AND CREAM DESSERT

Alexander I, like Peter the Great before him, imported a French chef, the great Antonin Carème. Carème named the new dish he created for the Czar after the dessert Apple Charlotte, which he had made for Charlotte, the only daughter of his former patron, George IV of England. Perhaps he was a little nostalgic for France and England (and Charlotte).

Serves 6

CAKE ROLL

3 *eggs, separated*   ⅓ *cup sifted flour*
⅓ *cup sugar*   ½ *cup raspberry preserves*

Heat the oven to moderate (350°F.). Butter a 15- by 10- by 1-inch jelly-roll pan and line it with wax paper; butter the paper. Turn egg whites into a medium-size bowl. With an electric beater at high speed, beat egg whites until foamy. Gradually beat in half the sugar, a little at a time and continue beating until egg whites form soft peaks. With the same beater, beat the egg yolks with the remaining sugar until thick and pale. Carefully fold the flour into the yolks. Fold the beaten egg whites carefully and thoroughly into the yolk mixture. Spread the batter evenly into the jelly-roll pan, using a spatula dipped in cold water from time to time. Smooth the top evenly. Bake for 12 minutes, or until center springs back when touched lightly with a fingertip. Spread a large kitchen towel on a countertop. Invert the baked cake on the towel. Gently peel off the wax paper. Cool almost completely. Carefully spread the raspberry preserves over the cake. Starting at the 15-inch side, roll up the cake jelly-roll fashion. Wrap the jelly roll in the towel and cool completely.

CREAM FILLING

3 *egg yolks*   1½ *cups milk*
½ *cup superfine sugar*   1½ *teaspoons vanilla*
1 *envelope (1 tablespoon)*   ¾ *cup heavy cream*
     unflavored gelatin   1 *tablespoon confectioner's sugar*

Beat the egg yolks lightly in a small bowl. In a medium-size saucepan, combine sugar and gelatin and mix well. Slowly stir in the milk and stir until mixture is smooth. Cook over medium heat, stirring constantly, only until mixture comes to the boiling point; do not boil. Stir ¼ cup gelatin-milk mixture into the yolks and blend thoroughly. Add yolks to the gelatin-milk in the saucepan and blend well. Cook over low heat, stirring constantly, until the mixture coats a wooden or silver spoon—about 5 minutes. Do not boil or the custard will curdle. (If the custard *has* curdled, push it through a fine sieve into a clean bowl.) Stir in vanilla. Chill in the refrigerator until the custard is beginning to thicken and forms a loose mound in a spoon. Beat the heavy cream until stiff; gradually beat in the confectioner's sugar. Fold the cream into the chilled, thickened custard and blend thoroughly.

TO ASSEMBLE CHARLOTTKA

Cut jelly roll into 24 even slices. Place 1 slice on the bottom of each of six 6-ounce custard cups. Place 3 slices upright on the sides of each custard cup. Spoon a scant ½ cup of Cream Filling into each of the jelly-roll lined custard cups. Smooth the top with a knife dipped in cold water. Cover with plastic wrap and chill for 4 to 5 hours, or until firm.

TO SERVE CHARLOTTKA

½ cup heavy cream
1 tablespoon confectioner's sugar

2 tablespoons minced pistachio nuts or finely chopped bitter chocolate

Beat the heavy cream until stiff; gradually beat in the confectioner's sugar. Run a knife around the edge of each custard cup to loosen the Charlottka. Invert on individual plates lined with a doily, or onto a serving platter lined with a doily. Decorate each Charlottka with a little whipped cream and sprinkle with 1 teaspoon pistachios or chocolate. Better still, pipe the whipped cream through a pastry bag with a rosette tip and then sprinkle with pistachios or chocolate.

Russian Cream

Russian cream has a lighter taste than ice cream—a marvelously airy consistency. It is a refreshing ending to a meal and much loved at the RTR.

Serves 6

½ cup water
4 envelopes unflavored gelatin
2 cups (1 pint) heavy cream
¼ cup sifted confectioner's sugar

1 drop red food coloring
1 quart vanilla ice cream, softened
⅓ cup slivered blanched almonds
⅓ cup grenadine syrup

Pour the water into a small bowl and sprinkle the gelatin over it. Stir to blend. Set the bowl in a pan of boiling water and dissolve the gelatin. While gelatin is dissolving, beat the cream until almost stiff. Beat in sugar gradually, a little at a time beating well after each addition. Do not overbeat. Stir the food coloring into the whipped cream. Cool the gelatin to lukewarm. Place the softened ice cream in a large bowl. With a wire whisk, beat the cooled gelatin into the soft ice cream. Fold in the whipped cream. Spoon equal amounts of the cream into 6 individual dessert dishes, or preferably, long-stemmed dessert glasses. Cover with plastic wrap and refrigerate for at least 4 hours. At serving time, sprinkle each dish with 1 tablespoon slivered almonds and top with 1 tablespoon grenadine syrup.

Cranberry Kissel

PURÉE OF CRANBERRIES SERVED WITH CREAM

Any berry or fruit can be used for kissel. The favorite in Russia is a berry resembling a gooseberry, unavailable here. Apples and apricots are favorites, too. In Scandinavia, cloudberries are much enjoyed in kissel. Kissel, as a dessert, because of its tartness and lightness, complements Chicken Kiev or Shashlik or any rich entree.

Serves 6

1¼ cups water
¼ cup sugar
1 can (16 ounces) jellied cranberry
     sauce

4 tablespoons cornstarch
   heavy cream

Pour ¾ cup of the water into a saucepan and bring to the boiling point. Stir in the sugar. Cook over medium heat, stirring constantly, until the sugar is dissolved. Stir in cranberry sauce. Cook over medium heat, stirring constantly, until the cranberry sauce is completely dissolved and the mixture smooth. Stir the cornstarch into the remaining ½ cup of water until mixture is smooth. Stir into the cranberries. Cook over low heat, stirring constantly, for 5 to 6 minutes, or until clear, thickened and smooth. Spoon into a glass serving dish or into 6 individual dessert dishes. Chill. Serve with heavy cream on the side.

Marzipan Potatoes

A BELOVED RUSSIAN TEA ROOM SPECIALTY FROM OUR TRAY OF HOME MADE PASTRIES

The Russian Tea Room Bakery is run as a separate entity inside the restaurant, with four full-time bakers under pastry chef Denis Candela turning out all our pastries, piroshki (which accompany every soup) and fantastic cakes by special order—and once a year Paska and Kulich by the ton. When I first came to The Russian Tea Room there were two bakers: "Papasha" Anakelian, an Armenian, and Willi Spaeth, a Bavarian. They worked side by side every day for over thirty years, and never could speak a single word to each other. Neither could they speak English—and once a "Happy Birthday Ellen" came with "Hold for Tuesday morning" spelled out on the cake! Denis's tribute in pastry to Sophia Loren caused a sensation at a recent party for her as it was wheeled into the Cafe, too large to be carried by hand.

Makes 12 "potatoes"

5 cups fine fresh chocolate cake crumbs (see below)
1 cup finely chopped walnuts
1 tablespoon rum or brandy
½ cup apricot preserves

2 8-ounce cans or two 7-ounce rolls almond paste, at room temperature
½ cup sifted cocoa

In a large bowl, combine chocolate cake crumbs, walnuts, rum or brandy and apricot preserves. Stir with a wooden spoon and blend thoroughly. Allowing about ¼ cup of the mixture for each ball, shape into 12 balls, using your hands. Reserve. Cut the almond paste into 12 equal pieces. If you are using 8-ounce cans, each piece will amount to approximately 2 tablespoons—less if you are using 7-ounce rolls. Place the almond-paste pieces between 2 sheets of wax paper and roll each out to a round measuring about 5 inches in diameter. Wrap each round of almond paste around 1 chocolate-cake-crumb ball. Tuck in and fold ends somewhat irregularly to imitate the shape of a potato. Place potatoes, seam side down, on a baking sheet and chill for 30 to 60 minutes to firm the almond paste. Roll each potato in the sifted cocoa. With the sharp end of a skewer, poke little holes in each potato to imitate potato eyes. Serve at room temperature.

TO MAKE CRUMBS

Tear Chocolate Cake (see below) into pieces. Seal inside a plastic bag, then roll with a rolling pin until the consistency of fine dry bread crumbs. Measure 5 cups for Marzipan Potatoes. Store any remaining chocolate crumbs in an airtight container for other uses.

CHOCOLATE CAKE

(for crumbs for Marzipan Potatoes or for eating as is)

1 *cup sifted cake flour*	2 *squares (1 ounce each)*
1 *cup sugar*	*unsweetened baking*
¼ *teaspoon baking powder*	*chocolate, chopped*
½ *teaspoon baking soda*	¼ *cup buttermilk*
½ *teaspoon salt*	1 *egg*
½ *cup water*	½ *teaspoon vanilla flavoring*

Preheat oven to moderate (350°F.). Butter and flour an 8-inch round cake pan. In a large bowl sift together flour, sugar, baking powder, baking soda and salt. Bring the water to the boiling point in a small saucepan. Add chopped chocolate. Cook over lowest possible heat, stirring constantly, only until chocolate has melted; be careful not to scorch the chocolate. Cool a little. Add the chocolate to the flour mixture, scraping the sides of the saucepan with a spatula. With an electric beater at high speed, beat for 1 minute or until blended. Combine buttermilk, egg and vanilla in a small bowl and beat together. Add to the chocolate mixture. Again using an electric beater at high speed, beat for 1 minute, or until smooth. Turn the batter into the prepared bake pan. Bake for 30 to 35 minutes or until cake tests clean and clears pan sides. Place on a cake rack and cool in the pan for 10 minutes. Then invert cake from pan on rack and cool thoroughly.

Note: If no buttermilk is available, add 1 teaspoon fresh lemon juice to ¼ cup milk.

Kasha à la Gourieff

A FAVORITE RUSSIAN DESSERT CONSISTING OF A FARINA PUDDING SERVED HOT OR COLD WITH FRUIT

Influenced by Swedish connections to Russian cuisine, Kasha à la Gourieff is served this way at The Russian Tea Room.

Serves 6

3 cups milk
1 cup light or heavy cream
⅓ cup sugar
⅓ cup farina or semolina or Cream of Wheat (not the quick-cooking kind)
2 tablespoons sweet butter
2 eggs, well beaten
¼ teaspoon vanilla

½ cup slivered blanched almonds, lightly toasted
1 to 1½ cups well-drained fresh, stewed or canned fruit such as cherries, thinly sliced peaches, pears or berries, mixed (the fruit should be ripe but firm)
Apricot Sauce (see below)

Combine milk and cream in a heavy saucepan. Add the sugar and bring to the boiling point. Lower heat. Add farina (or semolina or Cream of Wheat) slowly in a thin, steady stream, stirring with a wooden spoon as you do so. Cook over low heat, stirring constantly, for about 10 minutes, or until mixture is thickened and smooth. Stir in butter. Remove from heat and stir in eggs, mixing thoroughly. Stir in vanilla. Turn into a serving dish and sprinkle with the toasted almonds. Arrange fruit around the pudding. Serve warm with Apricot Sauce on the side.

Note: If to be served cold or chilled, cool before adding almonds and fruit.

APRICOT SAUCE

Makes about 1½ cups

1 cup apricot jam or preserves
2 teaspoons cornstarch
⅔ cup water

2 teaspoons fresh lemon juice, Kirsch or Cognac

Put the jam into a small, heavy saucepan. Cook over low heat, stirring constantly, until hot and melted. Remove from heat. Sprinkle cornstarch into the water and stir until smooth. Return saucepan to heat and stir in cornstarch mixture. Cook, stirring constantly, for 3 to 4 minutes, or until clear. Remove from heat and stir in lemon juice or Kirsch or Cognac. Turn into a sauceboat and serve hot with Kasha à la Gourieff.

VARIATION

Serves 6

3 *cups milk*
1 *cup light or heavy cream*
⅓ *cup sugar*
⅓ *cup farina or semolina or Cream of Wheat (not the quick-cooking kind)*
2 *tablespoons sweet butter*
2 *eggs, well beaten*
½ *cup finely grated blanched almonds*

1 *cup well-drained fresh, stewed or canned fruit such as cherries, thinly sliced peaches, pears or berries, mixed (the fruit should be firm), or 1 cup preserves*
2 *tablespoons sugar*
½ *cup slivered blanched almonds, toasted*
Apricot Sauce (see above)

Preheat oven to moderate (350°F.). Generously butter a deep 8-inch pie pan. Combine milk and cream in a heavy saucepan. Add the sugar and bring to the boiling point. Lower heat. Add farina (or semolina or Cream of Wheat) slowly in a thin, steady stream, stirring with a wooden spoon as you do so. Cook over low heat, stirring constantly, for about 10 minutes or until mixture is thickened and smooth. Stir in butter. Remove from heat and stir in eggs. Stir in the almonds. Spread half the pudding into the prepared pan and smooth it with a spatula dipped in cold water. Spread with fruit or preserves. Top with the remaining pudding and smooth the top with the spatula, again dipped in cold water. Bake for 10 to 15 minutes or until golden. Remove from oven and turn on broiler. Sprinkle the 2 tablespoons sugar evenly over the top of the pudding. Run quickly under hot broiler flame to caramelize the sugar to a light golden-brown color. Sprinkle with the toasted almonds and serve hot, with Apricot Sauce.

Strawberries Romanoff

One day Czar Alexander the First needed a sudden solution for a dessert, and Carême came up with what he had on hand—beautiful fresh strawberries with fresh cream—and then added ingredients that made it an inspired dessert.

Serves 6

3 *pints fresh ripe strawberries*
   dry white wine or water
   sugar to taste
   grated rind of 1 orange
⅓ *cup fresh orange juice*

⅔ *cup Curaçao*
2 *cups heavy cream*
¼ *cup confectioner's sugar*
¼ *teaspoon vanilla*

Stem the strawberries. Place them in a bowl and add enough dry white wine (or water) to cover to a height of 2 inches above the berries. Wash and swirl the strawberries quickly in the wine and drain. (Washing strawberries in dry white wine gives them added flavor; the wine need not be a premium wine.) Turn the strawberries into a deep serving dish; if they are large, halve or quarter them. Sprinkle with sugar to taste; amount depends on the sweetness of the berries. Toss with a fork. Sprinkle with orange rind, orange juice and Curaçao; toss with a fork again. Cover with plastic wrap and refrigerate for 2 to 4 hours, tossing the berries occasionally with a fork. At serving time, beat the cream until almost thick. Beat in the ¼ cup sugar and the vanilla. Beat until stiff, but do not overbeat. Spoon the whipped cream over the strawberries, or pipe it through a pastry bag fitted with a large fluted tube. Serve immediately.

Individual Crème Caramels

A CLASSIC FRENCH DESSERT ADOPTED BY THE RUSSIAN COURT IN THE NINETEENTH CENTURY

Serves 6 to 12

12 *custard cups*

CARAMEL

¾ *cup sugar*

CUSTARD

7 *eggs*	1 *teaspoon vanilla*
7 *egg yolks*	⅛ *teaspoon salt*
½ *cup superfine sugar*	5¼ *cups milk*

Preheat the oven to moderate (350°F.). Place custard cups on a baking sheet and into the oven to preheat; cold custard cups may crack when the hot caramel is poured into them. Turn the ¾ cup sugar into a small heavy saucepan. Cook over very low heat until the sugar has melted and is golden in color. Remove custard cups from oven. Spoon about 1 tablespoon melted sugar or caramel into each custard cup. Cool.

In a large bowl, beat together the eggs, egg yolks and sugar. Beat thoroughly, leaving no strands of unbeaten egg white. Beat in the vanilla and the salt. Heat the milk to scalding but do not boil. Gradually add the scalded milk to the egg mixture, beating all the time. If the egg-sugar mixture was not thoroughly blended, and you now see strands of unbeaten eggs floating in the custard, strain through a fine sieve. Pour about ⅔ cup custard into each cup, leaving about an ⅛-inch space at the cup's rim; custard will puff during baking. Set cups in a large, shallow baking pan and add enough warm water to the depth of 1 inch. Bake for about 45 minutes, or until a knife or a cake tester inserted in the center of the cup comes out clean. Remove at once from water bath and cool on a rack. Chill before serving. To unmold, run a knife quickly and carefully around the rims of the cups and invert on individual plates; the caramel will have covered the top of the custards and run down their sides. If desired, decorate with about 1 tablespoon sweetened whipped cream.

Mont Blanc of Chestnuts in Meringue Shells

Mont Blanc is one of the world's most luscious desserts—creamy chestnut purée topped with whipped cream. At The Russian Tea Room we serve our Mont Blanc in meringue shells, top it with whipped cream topped with chocolate curls or a chocolate drizzle, which, in its turn, is topped with a sprinkle of chopped pistachios. John Mazzola, president of Lincoln Center, loves this.

Makes 12 to 14 shells

NOTES ON MERINGUES

Many cooks think meringues are difficult to make, but this is not so at all if you keep a few things in mind. 1. Egg whites should be at room temperature before beating, because this makes for maximum volume. 2. Make sure that mixing bowl and egg beater are spotless and that there are no flecks of yolk in the whites. If so, fish them out with a piece of shell. Egg whites will not beat up if they, or the mixing bowl or the beaters contain any foreign matter, however small. 3. Superfine sugar is preferred to regular granulated because it dissolves more easily in beating. As you beat the egg whites, add the sugar very slowly, beating well after each addition, to dissolve it completely. If the sugar is not completely dissolved, "beads" or "tears" of syrup will form on the baked meringues. 4. Beat the egg whites and sugar thoroughly, but do not overbeat them. The meringue should be very stiff and glossy, but not dry, and it must not clump when spread. 5. You can beat meringues by hand, but it takes an incredible amount of effort. Use an electric beater or mixer but be careful not to overbeat. You'll get a larger volume with an electric beater than if you beat the meringue by hand.

NOTES ON MONT BLANC OF CHESTNUTS

Mont Blanc is a traditional European chestnut dessert, made in the fall and winter, when fresh chestnuts are in season. It is named after Europe's highest mountain, because, it is said, the brown of the chestnuts topped by the white of the whipped cream are reminiscent of the mountain's aspect. However, peeling, cooking and puréeing fresh chestnuts take a good deal of time and effort; besides, fresh chestnuts are seasonal. Canned chestnut purée, which is ready to use, makes an excellent substitute. Almost all canned chestnut purée is imported from France and is readily available in gourmet shops and in many supermarkets. There are two varieties: one plain and the other sweetened, and rather heavily so. Both kinds are rather dense and, we think, improved by a little whipped cream folded in to lighten them. The unsweetened purée obviously also needs sugar when used in desserts, though the flavor will not be as good as that of sweetened chestnut purée. The addition of a little rum, Kirsch, brandy or Crème de Cacao will improve the flavor of the sweetened purée, and will cut its sweetness as well.

When Mont Blanc is served in meringue shells, as in The Russian Tea Room, the crispness of the meringues forms a delicious contrast to the smoothness of the chestnut purée.

MERINGUE SHELLS

6 *egg whites (1 cup), at room temperature*	¼ *teaspoon cream of tartar*
⅛ *teaspoon salt*	1½ *cups superfine sugar*

Preheat the oven to low (200°F.). Lightly butter 2 large cookie sheets. Beat the egg whites with an electric beater or in an electric mixer until frothy. Add the salt and cream of tartar; these give beaten egg whites greater volume and stability. Beat in the sugar, 2 tablespoons at a time, beating well after each addition. Beat at highest speed until meringue is glossy and stiff enough to stand up straight when the beaters are withdrawn. Using a rounded ½-cup measure for each shell, and with the help of a teaspoon, drop the shells on the cookie sheets, leaving 2 to 3 inches of space between each shell to allow for expansion during baking. Shape each shell into a nest by using the spoon to make an indentation in the middle of the shell, which later will hold the filling. Dip the spoon frequently into cold water; this helps to prevent the meringue from sticking to the spoon when you are shaping both shells and nests. With a narrow spatula dipped in water as needed, smooth the exterior of the meringue nest as well as possible. Bake for 1½ hours for a firm and dried meringue. Turn off the oven, leave the oven door one-third open and let the meringue shells stand in the oven for 10 minutes to cool. Carefully lift the meringue shells off the cookie sheets with a broad spatula and cool completely. Place the meringue shells in airtight boxes until ready to use. Be sure the boxes close tightly, for humid air is a meringue's greatest enemy, making it elastic and apt to disintegrate. Fill with Chestnut Filling (below) at serving time. You may, however, keep filled meringue shells standing in a cool place for about 20 minutes; do not refrigerate.

MONT BLANC CHESTNUT FILLING

1 *square (1 ounce) semisweet chocolate*
1 *can (about 1 pound) imported sweetened chestnut purée*
1 *tablespoon rum, brandy or Crème de Cacao*

1½ *cups heavy cream*
2 *tablespoons shelled, minced pistachio nuts*

Place the chocolate in a small bowl or in the top of a small double boiler. Melt the chocolate over, not in, hot water. Remove from heat, but keep over hot water. Cover the chocolate to keep it soft and melted. Turn the chestnut purée into a big bowl and beat it with a wooden spoon to loosen it up and soften it. Beat in the rum or other liqueur. Measure ½ cup of the heavy cream into a small bowl and whip it until stiff. Do not overbeat or the cream will turn into butter. Fold the whipped cream into the chestnut purée. Beat the remaining cream until stiff. (It needs no sugar because the chestnut purée is very sweet.) Spoon equal amounts of the chestnut purée into the meringue shells, shaping it into little mounds. Cover the tops of the mounds with whipped cream to resemble a brown mountain capped with snow. With a demitasse spoon, drizzle a little of the melted chocolate over each cream-topped chestnut mound in its meringue shell. Top with a sprinkle of minced pistachios and serve as soon as possible.

Chocolate Mousse

Serves 6

3 *squares (1 ounce each)*
      semisweet chocolate
3 *squares (1 ounce each)*
      unsweetened chocolate
2 *tablespoons hot water*

5 *eggs, separated*
1½ *teaspoons vanilla*
1½ *cups heavy cream*
2 *tablespoons rum or brandy or*
      Kirsch

FOR DECORATION

½ *cup heavy cream*
   chocolate curls made from 3
      squares semisweet or
      unsweetened chocolate

Combine semisweet and unsweetened chocolate and hot water in the top of a double boiler. Set over simmering, not boiling, water. Over low heat, stir until the chocolate has melted and is smooth. Remove from heat. Beat the egg yolks with a fork and add 2 or 3 tablespoons of the chocolate to the beaten yolks. Mix well. Pour the egg-yolk mixture back into the top of the double boiler containing the chocolate. Mix thoroughly. Set double-boiler top again over bottom containing simmering water. Cook over low heat, stirring constantly, for 3 to 4 minutes; do not boil. Cool. Stir in vanilla and the rum, brandy or Kirsch. Whip the 1½ cups cream and fold it into the chocolate mixture. Beat the egg whites until stiff but not dry and fold them gently and quickly into the chocolate-cream mixture. Spoon equal amounts of the mixture into six 6-ounce individual dishes or custard cups. Cover with plastic wrap. Chill for 12 hours or overnight, until firm. At serving time, whip the ½ cup heavy cream until stiff. Spoon a little cream on each individual mousse and top with chocolate curls.

TO MAKE CHOCOLATE CURLS

With a vegetable peeler or a small, sharp knife shave chocolate in long thin strokes to form curls. Shave directly over individual mousses or onto wax paper first.

Baba au Rhum

*Makes 12 babas
or one large 1½-quart baba*

DOUGH

6 tablespoons lukewarm water
  (105 to 115°F)
1 envelope dry active yeast
1 teaspoon salt
6 tablespoons sugar
6 tablespoons lukewarm milk (105
  to 115°F)

½ cup butter, melted and cooled
5 eggs
  grated rind of 1 orange or lemon
3 cups sifted flour

Pour the water into a large bowl and sprinkle the yeast over it. Stir to dissolve yeast. Stir in salt, sugar, milk, butter, eggs and orange or lemon rind. Beat until smooth. Beat in flour gradually, 10 minutes by hand, or 2 minutes with an electric beater at medium speed. The batter will be smooth and shiny. Cover the bowl with a damp kitchen towel and let rise in a warm, draft-free place until doubled in bulk, or for about 1 hour. While the dough is rising, generously butter twelve 6-ounce custard cups or large muffin pans, or 1½-quart ring mold. Beat the risen dough for 2 minutes and turn it in equal amounts into the prepared cups (or pans or mold). The pans or mold will be half full. Let rise without a cover in a warm, draft-free place until doubled in bulk, or for 30 to 35 minutes. The dough will come to the top of the pans or mold. While dough is rising, preheat the oven to hot (425°F.). Bake the small babas for 10 to 12 minutes and the large baba for 25 to 30 minutes, or until cakes test clean. While the babas are baking, prepare the Rhum Syrup.

RHUM SYRUP

2½ cups sugar
 2 cups water

½ cup dark rum
1 teaspoon rum extract

Combine sugar and water in a saucepan. Bring to the boiling point and simmer over low heat without a cover for 10 minutes. Remove from the heat and stir in rum and rum extract. Allow to cool slightly; the syrup should be warm when poured over the cake.

TO ASSEMBLE BABAS

Run a knife around the edge of each baba cup (or the ring mold) to loosen the cake. Unmold into a large bowl. Pour the warm syrup over the babas. Let babas stand at room temperature in the syrup, turning them occasionally and basting them frequently or until most of the syrup has been absorbed by the cakes. With a slotted spoon, lift babas from bowl. Place babas on a rack standing on a platter and let them drain. While babas are draining, prepare the Glaze.

GLAZE

½ cup apricot preserves
2 tablespoons lemon juice

Strain the apricot preserves through a sieve into a small saucepan. Stir in lemon juice. Over medium heat, warm the mixture until bubbly. With a pastry brush, brush the warm glaze over the babas, covering them on all sides. Cool. Close to serving time, place the babas on a platter lined with doilies and prepare the Topping (below).

TOPPING

1 cup heavy cream
2 tablespoons confectioner's sugar
1 teaspoon vanilla

Beat the cream until almost stiff and beat in the sugar, one tablespoon at a time. Add vanilla and beat until stiff. Spoon whipped cream into a pastry bag with a star tip and press large rosettes of whipped cream on each baba. Chill until ready to serve; serve as soon as possible.

Sacher Torte

From the Hotel Sacher in Vienna came one of the world's most famous pastries, and no classic pastry tray is complete without it. In Vienna, the Sacher hotel sends vans around the city delivering these delectables.

1 8-inch square cake; in 3 layers

Serves 10 to 12

6 eggs, separated, at room
    temperature
½ cup sugar
½ cup butter, at room temperature

1 package (6 ounces) semisweet
    chocolate pieces, melted and
    cooled
¾ cup sifted cake flour
1 teaspoon baking powder
½ cup raspberry preserves

Preheat oven to low-moderate (325°F.). Butter an 8-inch-square baking pan. Line the bottom with wax paper and butter the paper. In a large bowl, with an electric beater at high speed, beat the egg whites until foamy. Gradually beat in ⅓ cup of the sugar, 1 tablespoon at a time, beating well after each addition. Beat until stiff but not dry. Put the butter in another large bowl. With the same beater, beat the butter until very soft and creamy. Beat in the remaining sugar. Beat in the egg yolks, 2 at a time, beating well after each addition. Stir in the melted chocolate and mix thoroughly until all the chocolate has been incorporated into the egg mixture. Fold the beaten egg whites carefully and gently into the chocolate mixture. Hold a strainer or sieve over the bowl with the batter and put the flour and baking powder into it. Sift the flour carefully over the batter and fold it in gently, just until blended. Turn into the prepared baking pan. Bake for 1¼ hours, or until the cake tests clean. Cool the cake in its pan, set on a wire cake rack for 10 minutes. With a knife, loosen the edges carefully and unmold the cake by inverting on rack. Carefully peel off the wax paper. Cool the cake completely. Measure the height of the cake, and with toothpicks stuck in a side of the cake, mark off 3 equal layers. Using the toothpicks to guide you, cut the cake into 3 layers with a very sharp knife. Sandwich the layers together with the raspberry preserves. Brush off any crumbs and place the cake on a sheet of wax paper, ready to frost with Chocolate Glaze.

CHOCOLATE GLAZE

Makes about 1 cup

2 *tablespoons water*	1½ *squares (1½ ounces)*
2 *tablespoons light corn syrup*	*unsweetened baking*
1½ *cups sifted confectioner's sugar*	*chocolate, chopped*

Combine all the ingredients in a small bowl and mix thoroughly until reasonably smooth. Set the bowl in a pan with simmering, not boiling, water placed over low heat. Stir constantly until the chocolate has melted and the glaze is thin enough for frosting the cake.

To frost, spoon the Chocolate Glaze over the top of the cake, letting it drip down on the sides. Smooth the glaze with a spatula dipped in warm water, making sure that the top of the cake is well covered. When the glaze is firm, cut the cake into portions and serve.

Walnut Cake

Walnuts are the favorite nuts used in Russian cooking. In Georgia, where walnuts are plentiful, they are used in many unusual dishes and sauces and even to accompany fish dishes. Almond paste is sold generally either in 8-ounce cans or 7-ounce rolls. Either may be used for this cake, as the slight weight difference does not affect results.

Makes one 9-inch square cake in 2 layers

6 *eggs, separated*
¼ *teaspoon salt*
½ *cup sugar*
    One 8-ounce can (or 7-ounce roll) almond paste, crumbled

½ *teaspoon vanilla extract*
1 *cup ground walnuts (1½ cups walnut pieces)*
½ *cup fine dry breadcrumbs*

Preheat the oven to moderate (350°F.). Butter two 9-inch square baking pans. Line the bottoms with wax paper and butter the paper. In a large bowl, with an electric beater, beat the egg whites until foamy. Add the salt and beat until soft peaks are beginning to form. Gradually beat in the sugar, 1 tablespoon at a time, beating well after each addition. Beat for 3 to 5 more minutes or until mixture is very stiff. In a large bowl, with the same beater, beat the egg yolks until thick and pale. Beat in the almond paste, a little at a time and beat until mixture is creamy and thoroughly blended. Fold in the walnuts and the breadcrumbs. Mix well. Carefully fold in the egg whites only until blended. Spoon equal amounts of the batter into the 2 pans. Bake for 35 to 40 minutes, or until the cake shrinks from the sides of the pan and springs back when touched lightly with your finger. Place the cake pans on wire cake racks and let the cakes cool in the pans for 10 minutes. Gently invert the cakes on the racks and peel off the wax paper. Cool thoroughly. Place on a large platter.

SUGAR SYRUP

¼ *cup sugar*
½ *cup water*
2 *tablespoons brandy or rum*

Combine all the ingredients in a small saucepan. Over medium heat, cook uncovered for 5 minutes; cool. Reserve.

ALMOND LATTICE TOP

One 8-ounce can (or 7-ounce roll) almond paste, crumbled

1 *egg white*
¼ *cup sugar*

Combine all ingredients in a small bowl. Beat at high speed with an electric beater or mixer until creamy and thoroughly blended. Turn mixture into a pastry bag with a small plain tube.

TO ASSEMBLE WALNUT CAKE

1 *cup apricot preserves*

Preheat the oven to moderate (350° F.). Brush the soft sides of the 2 layers with the sugar syrup. Spread 1 layer with ½ cup of the apricot preserves, smoothing the top with a knife dipped in cold water. Place the other layer on top of the preserves. Pipe a lattice pattern of 6 or 7 strips of almond paste, each ¼ inch wide, lengthwise and crosswise over the cake and attach them loosely to the cake edge to allow for shrinkage. Moisten the ends slightly to make them stick. Neatly cut off any strips that are too long. For a shinier lattice top, brush the strips with milk. Place the cake on a buttered and floured baking sheet. Bake for about 15 minutes or until lattice top is golden brown. Cool the cake slightly. Fill the spaces between the lattice strips with the remaining apricot preserves. Cool thoroughly. To serve, cut the cake into 1- to 1¼-inch-thick slices.

Chocolate-Covered Eclairs

Though Napoleon lost Moscow he made a mark with the introduction of the Eclair and the Napoleon in Russia.

Makes 12 eclairs

ECLAIRS

1 *cup water*
½ *cup butter, cut into pieces*
1 *teaspoon sugar*
¼ *teaspoon salt*
1 *cup sifted flour*
4 *eggs, at room temperature*

Preheat oven to hot (400°F.). Combine water, butter, sugar and salt in a large saucepan. Bring to a rolling boil over medium heat. Add the flour *all at once*. Stir vigorously with a wooden spoon for about 1 minute or until the mixture forms a ball that leaves the sides of the saucepan clean. Remove from heat. Using a wooden spoon, beat in eggs, one at a time, beating vigorously after each addition. Beat until the dough is smooth and shiny. Attach a large plain tip to a pastry bag, or use the bag without a tip. Spoon dough into bag. On an ungreased baking sheet, press out twelve 4-inch-long and 1-inch-wide strips. Leave 2 inches of space between strips. Bake for 40 to 45 minutes, or until puffed and golden brown. With a wide spatula, transfer baked eclairs to wire cake racks. Cool completely.

Note: Instead of using a pastry bag, drop dough by rounded tablespoonfuls on the baking sheet to make 12 equal-size mounds. The mounds should be 2 inches apart, in rows that should be 6 inches apart. With a teaspoon and a spatula dipped occasionally into cold water, shape each mound into an oval measuring 4 by 1 by 1 inches. Bake as above.

FILLING

3 *eggs, at room temperature*
½ *cup sugar*
⅓ *cup cornstarch*
2 *cups milk*
1 *teaspoon vanilla extract*

Break the eggs into a medium-size saucepan and beat until foamy. Sift together the sugar and the cornstarch. Beat mixture gradually into beaten eggs, beating until smooth. Scald the milk but do not boil it. Stir the scalded milk slowly into the egg mixture, stirring constantly as you do this. Cook over medium heat, stirring all the time, for 3 to 4 minutes, or until thickened and smooth. Remove from heat and stir in vanilla. Cover the saucepan and chill for 2 to 3 hours in the refrigerator.

TO FILL ECLAIRS

Using the point of a skewer or a small sharp knife, make 3 small holes in the flat underside of each eclair. Turn filling into a pastry bag with a small tube. Invert. Press filling into the holes of the eclairs to fill them. Or cut eclairs into halves lengthwise. If there is any soft dough inside, pull it out gently. Fill; replace tops. Place the eclairs on wire racks set over pieces of wax paper before icing them with Chocolate Glaze.

CHOCOLATE GLAZE

1 *square (1 ounce) unsweetened chocolate*
1 *tablespoon butter, at room temperature*

2 *tablespoons water*
1 *cup sifted confectioner's sugar*
1 *teaspoon vanilla*

Combine chocolate, butter and water in a small bowl. Place the bowl in a pan with simmering (not boiling) water. Stir constantly until chocolate and butter are melted and mixture is smooth. Remove bowl from heat. Beat in confectioner's sugar and vanilla, beating until smooth. *While the glaze is still warm,* spoon a little over each filled eclair, letting the mixture run down the sides of the eclairs. Serve within 2 hours for optimum flavor.

Important! Do *not* refrigerate eclairs or they will get soggy.

Eight-Layer Cake

A seven-layer cake is an American tradition that we follow at The Russian Tea Room. However, for home bakers it is easier to make an eight-layer cake. And what's wrong with an extra layer of delicious cake?

Makes one 10- by 40-inch cake

Serves 12

5 large eggs, separated
⅔ cup sugar, preferably superfine
1 teaspoon orange or vanilla
       extract

⅔ cup sifted cake flour
    Butter Cream Filling (see below)
    Chocolate Frosting (see below)

Preheat the oven to moderate (350°F.). Generously butter two 15- by 10- by 1-inch jelly-roll pans. Line each pan with wax paper. Butter the paper. In a large bowl, beat the egg whites, preferably with an electric beater, until foamy. Add ⅓ cup of the sugar, 1 tablespoon at a time, beating well after each addition. Beat until stiff but not dry (egg whites should form a soft-peaked meringue). In another large bowl, with the same beaters, beat the egg yolks with the remaining ⅓ cup of the sugar until thick and light. Beat in orange or vanilla extract. Sift ⅓ of the sifted cake flour over the egg-yolk mixture. Fold it in quickly but gently. Repeat with remaining flour. Fold half of the beaten egg whites into the beaten egg-yolk mixture. Fold this into the remaining beaten egg whites. Spread half the batter evenly into each prepared jelly-roll pan. Smooth the tops with a spatula dipped quickly in cold water. Bake for 12 minutes or until the center of each cake springs back when lightly touched with a fingertip. While cakes are baking, spread clean kitchen towels on countertop or table. They should form a large enough surface to hold both baked jelly rolls. Invert each roll onto a clean kitchen-towel surface. Carefully peel off the wax paper. Cool completely. Cut each cooled cake into 4 strips, each measuring about 10 by 4 inches. Put the strips together with Butter Cream Filling as you would a layer cake, but leave top strip bare. Frost top and sides of the cake with the Chocolate Frosting. Chill the cake for at least 2 hours, or overnight, before serving.

BUTTER CREAM FILLING

Makes 1½ cups

½ cup sweet butter, at room
    temperature
1 egg yolk

2¾ cups sifted confectioner's sugar
3 teaspoons instant coffee powder
⅓ cup cold water

In a medium-size bowl, cream the butter until it is soft. Beat in the egg yolk and 1 cup of the confectioner's sugar. Stir the instant coffee in the water until dissolved. Beat remaining sugar and the coffee alternately into the butter mixture, beginning and ending with confectioner's sugar. Use immediately to fill the cake.

CHOCOLATE FROSTING

Makes 2½ to 3 cups

4 squares (4 ounces) unsweetened
    chocolate
1 cup butter, at room
    temperature, cut into pieces
2 egg yolks, beaten

2½ to 3 cups sifted confectioner's
    sugar
½ cup light cream
1 tablespoon vanilla

Put the chocolate into the top of a double boiler. Melt the chocolate over hot, not boiling, water, stirring occasionally until smooth. Remove from heat. Beat in the butter, a little at a time, beating well after each addition. Beat in egg yolks and blend thoroughly. Beat in 2½ cups confectioner's sugar alternately with the light cream, until mixture is smooth and of spreading consistency. If necessary, beat in more sugar, 1 tablespoon at a time, for proper spreading consistency. Beat in vanilla. If frosting is too soft, chill for 15 minutes before frosting the sides and top of the cake.

Puff Pastry

Homemade puff pastry is so much better than the commercial product that it is worthwhile to make it. But it will never rise as high as commerical puff pastry because the latter is made with a special pastry flour. Puff pastry consists of many thin layers of dough separated by many layers of thin butter. In baking, the butter melts and creates steam, which makes the pastry rise, and the melted butter crisps the layers of dough. Puff pastry must be made with very cold ingredients. Don't try it when the weather is hot and humid. At The Russian Tea Room, puff pastry is the base of many desserts and also of piroshki.

Makes about 2½ pounds

4 *cups sifted all-purpose flour*	1⅓ *to 1½ cups cold water*
2 *tablespoons cornstarch*	1 *pound sweet butter*
1½ *teaspoons salt*	

In a large bowl, combine the flour, cornstarch and salt and mix together. Make a hole in the center of the flour mixture and add 1⅓ cups of the water. With your finger, stir the flour gradually into the water. Stir until all the flour is moistened and forms large clumps of dough. Since different flours absorb water differently, you may have to add more water, 1 tablespoon at a time. Knead the dough with a few strokes into a ball that will look lumpy; do not overwork the dough. Place the ball of dough on a plate that has been floured to prevent sticking. With a sharp knife, cut a cross halfway through the thickness of the ball of dough. Refrigerate, uncovered, for 30 minutes. While the dough is chilling, unwrap the butter and let it stand at room temperature for 5 minutes. Fill a bowl with ice and water and chill your hands in the water. Cut the butter quickly into ½-inch-thick slices. With your chilled hands, knead the butter into a large, waxy ball. Chill your hands frequently to keep the butter firm, cold and waxy, like clay. Place a sheet of wax paper on your working surface and pat the butter into an 8-inch square. Chill the butter about 30 minutes or until it has the same consistency as the dough—this is important. If the butter is too hard, it will pierce the dough, and if the dough is too hard, it will squeeze out the butter during rolling.

Flour your working surface heavily so that the dough will not stick. Place the ball of dough, cross side up, on the floured surface. With your chilled hands, pat it into an 8-inch square. Place the square of butter *diagonally* on the square of dough. The 4 points of the butter square should center the 4 sides of the dough square. Fold the dough over the butter so that the corners of the dough square meet in the center of the butter square. The mixture should now look like the back of an envelope. Press down lightly on the edges to seal them and let the mixture rest for 5 minutes. With a floured rolling pin, and using as few strokes as possible, roll the dough gently into a 9- by 18-inch oblong. Roll *up* from the center of the dough for 9 inches and then roll *down* from the center of the dough for 9 inches. Make sure that the width of the dough is always 9 inches. If not, tap in the sides to keep it so. Always roll the dough from the middle up or down, and in such a way that the dough is even. It should be about ½ inch thick. Be careful not to press down on the edges of the dough as this will cause the enclosed butter to ooze out. (Keep your working surface well floured each time the dough is rolled; it must not stick.) Too much rolling results in a tough, heavy puff paste. Fold the dough oblong lengthwise into thirds. As you fold the dough, brush off excess flour with a pastry brush; too much flour also toughens the puff paste. Turn the folded dough around so that it looks like a book ready to be opened. In the manner described above, quickly roll the dough again into a 9- by 18-inch oblong. Fold again, brushing off excess flour. (Your dough has now been given 2 turns.) Place the dough on a floured plate, cover with foil and chill in the refrigerator for 1 hour. Repeat the rolling out and folding procedure two more times, chilling the dough once between rolling and folding. After the last folding, dust the entire dough with flour, wrap it in foil and chill overnight. The dough must be thoroughly chilled before baking.

Note: It is important to make the amount of puff pastry specified in this recipe; making smaller amounts does not give good results. This puff-pastry dough is best stored well wrapped in the freezer. Long storage in the refrigerator causes the dough to darken in color. The dough may be cut into smaller portions for freezing. Thaw in its wrapping overnight for use as needed. When baking puff pastry, to avoid a messy clean-up line the bottom of the oven with foil to catch any buttery drippings.

Napoleons

Makes 12 pastries

PASTRY CREAM

6 *egg yolks*
¼ *cup cornstarch*
½ *cup sugar*

2 *cups half and half or light cream*
2 *teaspoons vanilla*

FROSTING

2 *cups sifted confectioner's sugar*
2 *to 3 tablespoons milk*
1 *teaspoon vanilla*

CHOCOLATE GLAZE

1 *ounce (1 square) semisweet chocolate*
1 *teaspoon vegetable shortening*

1 *recipe Puff Pastry (page 210) (if frozen, thawed)*

Use a glass, Teflon or enameled saucepan for making the Pastry Cream because a metal saucepan will discolor it and give it a greenish tinge.

In a small heavy saucepan or the top of a double boiler, beat the egg yolks. Stir in the cornstarch and beat until smooth. Stir in sugar, beat again, and then stir in the half and half or light cream. Preferably with a wire whisk, beat until the mixture is smooth and free of lumps. Over very low heat, or over simmering, not boiling, water, and stirring constantly, cook the custard until it thickens. Do not let it boil. Remove pan from heat and set the pan in a large bowl. Fill the bowl with ice cubes, making sure that the pan is well surrounded by them. Stir

constantly until the custard is cold. Stir in vanilla. Let the custard stay on the ice, taking care that no water from the melting ice gets into it.

For the Frosting, pour the confectioner's sugar into a small bowl. Stir in 2 tablespoons of the milk and the vanilla, and beat until smooth. If too thick, add, one teaspoon at a time, the remaining milk, stirring until smooth and of spreading consistency. Cover with wax paper or a clean kitchen towel to prevent the frosting from drying out.

For the Chocolate Glaze, combine the chocolate and the shortening in a small bowl or in the top of a small double boiler. Over hot, not boiling, water, stir mixture until the chocolate is melted and the mixture is smooth. Remove from heat, but keep bowl with chocolate mixture over hot water until ready to use.

Cut the Puff Pastry into 2 pieces. On a well-floured working surface, roll out each piece into a 12- by 17-inch oblong. Place each oblong on an ungreased cookie sheet and trim the ragged edges. Make sure that the two oblongs are exactly the same size. Prick the doughs with a fork 3 or 4 times. Chill for 1 hour in the refrigerator. Preheat the oven to hot (425°F.). Bake for 18 to 20 minutes, or until golden brown and crisp. Cool sheets on a rack.

When ready to assemble the Napoleons, with a serrated knife and using a sewing motion cut each piece of cooled pastry (leaving it on its cookie sheet) into 18 pieces, each measuring 2 by 4 inches. Spread 24 of the pieces evenly with Pastry Cream. Sandwich these by placing 1 piece on top of another to make 12 pastries—the top piece should be cream side up. Spread the top of the remaining 12 pieces evenly with Frosting. Drizzle the Chocolate Glaze back and forth over the Frosting on each pastry. To make the traditional spiderweb design, draw the tip of a small pointed knife across the Chocolate Glaze, first in one direction and then the other. Top the cream-filled pastries with these 12 frosted pieces. With a wide spatula, remove Napoleons carefully from the cookie sheets. Transfer to a serving dish and serve as soon as possible.

Baklava

Our guests delight in this crisp, wonderfully rich Middle Eastern pastry, made from chopped nuts and gossamer phyllo pastry sheets and steeped in a honeyed syrup. Phyllo pastry sheets, as thin as the skin of an onion, are widely used in Greek and Middle Eastern cooking. Frozen, they can be found in many supermarkets, gourmet shops and Middle Eastern groceries. Before being used, frozen phyllo sheets must be thawed to room temperature because when cold they break easily. Miss Jean Dalrymple, doyenne of the City Center in New York, is a devoted fan of baklava.

Makes 20 to 24 pastries

FILLING

1 *pound (4 cups) shelled walnuts,*
        coarsely ground
½ *cup superfine sugar*

1 *teaspoon grated lemon rind*
1 *teaspoon ground cinnamon*

PHYLLO PASTRY

1 *pound phyllo pastry sheets*
        (about thirty 12- by
        17-inch sheets)

1½ *cups (¾ pound) butter,*
        melted and cooled

SYRUP

1½ *cups sugar*
1½ *cups water*
¼ *cup honey*

1 *tablespoon fresh lemon*
        juice

TO MAKE THE FILLING

Combine all the ingredients in a large bowl and mix thoroughly. If you are using a food processor, combine the shelled (but not ground) walnuts with the sugar, lemon rind and cinnamon in the bowl of the processor. Process to desired consistency. Reserve.

ASSEMBLING AND BAKING THE PHYLLO

Preheat the oven to moderate (350°F.). Lay the phyllo pastry sheets on a lightly floured surface. If they are rolled up, unroll them and open them up so that they are completely flat. Using a baking pan that is 12 by 8 by 2 inches or 13 by 9 by 2 inches, coat the bottom and sides with 1 tablespoon of the butter. Use a pastry brush for this. Brush ½ (one end) of a phyllo sheet with butter. Fold the sheet in half crosswise, lift it up carefully and place it in the bottom of the pan. Butter the top side of the folded phyllo sheet. Repeat this procedure for 9 more phyllo sheets. You now have used 10 phyllo sheets. Each folded sheet makes 2 layers, so that now you have 20 layers of phyllo sheet pastry, stacked one on top of the other. Spread half of the filling over the phyllo sheets in the pan. Repeat the same procedure using 10 more buttered phyllo sheets, placing these on top of the first stack. Spread the remaining half of the filling over the phyllo pastry. Top the filling with the remaining 10 phyllo sheets, buttering and folding them as described. This is the order in the pan:

10 folded and buttered phyllo sheets
½ the filling
10 folded and buttered phyllo sheets
½ the filling
10 folded and buttered phyllo sheets

Butter the top layer of phyllo sheets very liberally; if necessary, use 2 to 4 more tablespoons melted and cooled butter.

With the point of a small, sharp knife score the top of the pastry with parallel diagonal lines about 2 inches apart and ½-inch deep. Cross these diagonally to make the traditional diamond shapes into which they will later be cut. Since diamond-shape pastries produce a certain amount of wasted pastry at the edges of the pan, you may avoid this waste by making 3 vertical and 5 horizontal cuts in the pastry, which will produce squares. Place the pan with the baklava on the center rack of the oven. Bake for 30 minutes. Turn the heat down to low (300°F.) and bake for 45 minutes longer, or until the top is golden brown and crisp.

While the pastry is baking, make the Syrup: Combine sugar, water and honey in a small heavy saucepan. Bring to the boiling point over medium heat. Turn heat to low. Simmer for 15 minutes. Remove from heat and stir in the lemon juice. Pour the hot syrup over the baked baklava. Cool to room temperature. Just before serving, cut the baklava into pieces.

Tea and Coffee

Tea came to Russia by way of China, and though there is a large tea production in Georgia and the Crimea (black, very strong tea), "Russian Tea" is actually a blend of Ceylon and Indian teas. The Russian Tea Room tea is a special blend of these teas with spices, and we buy the blend in large chests. It has great flavor and aroma, and we serve it in the classic Russian style—in a glass, with cherry preserves, (about ½ cup of preserves—in a little side dish). These are then spooned into the tea glasses by our guests.

Tea and the special coffees that follow are served Russian fashion in 8-ounce glasses set in metal holders with a handle. Regular coffee is served in coffee cups and espresso in demitasse cups. We serve hot tea plain, with sugar, cream, honey or lemon, or with about 1¼ ounces (a shot-glassful) of vodka or dark rum. Of course you may wish to vary the amounts of spirits added to tea or to our special coffees to suit your own taste.

Our special coffees are delicious. Cafe Russe mates with a shot-glassful of vodka; Cafe Royal with the same amount of brandy; and Coffee Vienna is topped with a mound of snowy whipped cream. Irish Coffee is made the classic way, with sweetened coffee strengthened with about 1¼ ounces of Irish whiskey and topped with a cloud of whipped cream. We add about ⅓ cup strong hot coffee to Hot Chocolate à la Russe to give it a mocha flavor, and we float very generous amounts of whipped cream in it. The noblest of our chocolate drinks, and the favorite of the late great Russian singer Feodor Chaliapin, is our Hot Chocolate Chaliapin, enlivened by about 1¼ ounces of vodka and with coffee liqueur and whipped cream.

Any of these special drinks will send you off to the concert in a great mood; and your guests at home will have a marvelous time experimenting with these usual and unusual coffee and tea recipes to complete an adventurous meal.

DRINKS
AT THE
RUSSIAN
TEA ROOM

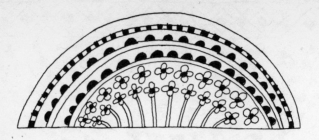

The Russian Tea Room has two extraordinary bars—the dining room bar, where people have a drink while waiting for friends or for their table, and the more intimate Café bar upstairs, where they can sit and drink at leisure. Vodka reigns supreme, and The Russian Tea Room Vodka outsells all other vodkas by far.

Vodkas · RTR Vodka Drinks · Wines

Vodka

Vladimir, the early Russian ruler, rejected the Moslem religion in favor of Christianity because, he said, "The joy of Russia is drinking— she cannot do without it!" As we all know, vodka became king of Russian drinks because it can be made from potatoes, sugar cane, grain, beets or chemicals, any process that ends up being pure alcohol and water—"natural spirits."

One of the joys of vodka is its ability to combine with so many mixers; it doesn't bring an overpowering taste when added to orange juice, tomato juice, tonic, vermouth, almost anything one might fancy in a mixed drink. Another great quality of vodka is that it can be flavored with a number of fascinating ingredients, such as buffalo grass, and it then becomes Zubrovka—a marvelous taste. When fresh peppercorns are put in a bottle of vodka for a few days we have Petsovka. A lemon peel inserted in the bottle on a string and removed after a couple of days makes a delicious lemon vodka; or you can use an orange peel, anise seeds, pitted cherries, a tea bag, caraway seeds — anything your taste buds desire!

Russians never drink without eating or eat without drinking—and the numerous toasts given and drunk down neatly in a thimble-sized glass are always accompanied by food, usually from an enormous zakuska table full of hot and cold hors d'oeuvres. Vodka is the perfect accompaniment to zakuska, and especially to caviar, as the purity of its taste enhances the special taste sensations of sturgeon roe. The vodka itself will only be noticed as an aftertaste.

The Russian Tea Room has its own vodka our label chosen from an original woodcut by the great nineteenth-century Russian painter Bilibin in The Russian Tea Room collection. The scene on the label is a view of old Moscow and the Kremlin spires seen from the river below that winds around the city walls. The Russian Tea Room sells more vodka than any other single restaurant in America. We feature, besides The Russian Tea Room Vodka, twenty different imported vodkas from as many countries around the world.

The Russian Tea Room Vodka Cocktail List has become a classic, and many guests keep asking for their favorite drinks throughout the years. For your convenience in re-creating these drinks at home, we give you the exact recipes below. Several Russian celebrities have had drinks named after them that appear on The Russian Tea Room Vodka Cocktail List, including Chaliapin and Nureyev. One drink you *won't* find on our list is a fantastic creation by Milton Glaser, inspired by his marvelous RTR postcard drawings. You must have "The Rasputin!" he cried, as he feverishly jotted down on a Russian Tea Room cocktail napkin, "One part Stolichnaya . . . three parts clam juice . . . one anchovy . . . one olive." Sad to say, we were the only people who ever ordered it. But what courage!

The Boyar, the Katinka, the Dyevitchka, all bring back such happy memories to us—of dancers and musicians and artists we've seen over the years in The Russian Tea Room—and with whom we've many times shared a *Nazdarovya!*. A party we gave for the cast of *The Cherry Orchard*, for instance, when it was revived in the seventies at Lincoln Center with Irene Worth, Raul Julia, George Voskovic and others. Our Japanese chef Tsuyoshi made a marvelous ice carving of a cherry tree; in the center was a frozen bottle of vodka which was removed and served. It was a very Russian evening, and everyone took on his Chekhovian role more and more as the hour grew later.

One other memory—the Czar's officers had their annual reunion in the Boyar Room of The Russian Tea Room as long as they could still get into their uniforms and travel to New York City from wherever they lived. They would order and consume in a few hours two bottles of vodka apiece! And they always got to their feet and marched out at the end of the evening solemnly saluting Anatole, then our maitre d' and a former member of the Czar's cadet corps.

RTR Vodka Drinks

All our drinks are served on ice.

Ballet Russe
  1 ounce vodka; 2½ ounces fresh, sweetened lemon juice; ½ ounce crème de cassis— shake.

Black Russian
  2 ounces vodka; 1½ ounces Kahlua.

Bolshoi Punch
  1 ounce vodka; 2½ ounces fresh, sweetened lemon juice; ¼ ounce rum; ¼ ounce crème de cassis—shake.

Boyar Imperiale
  2 ounces Russian vodka; 1½ ounces Cherry Heering.

Dyevitchka
  1 ounce vodka; ½ ounce Triple Sec; 1½ ounces fresh, sweetened lemon juice; ½ ounce pineapple juice—shake.

Nureyev
2 ounces vodka; 1½ ounces white crème de cacao.

Ochi Chernya
2 ounces vodka; ¼ ounce dry vermouth; ¼ ounce sweet vermouth; black olive.

Pavlova
1½ ounces vodka; 1 ounce white crème de cacao; 1 ounce cream.

Pushkin
1 ounce vodka; 1 ounce gin; 1 ounces white crème de cacao.

Boyar Imperiale
2 ounces Russian vodka; 1½ ounce Cherry Heering.

Gorki
2½ ounces vodka; ½ ounce Benedictine; 2 dashes of bitters.

Ivan the Terrible
2 ounces vodka; 1½ ounces green chartreuse.

Katinka
1 ounce vodka; 2½ ounces fresh, sweetened lemon juice; ½ ounce apricot liqueur—shake.

Moscow Mule RTR
1½ ounces vodka; slice of lime; 3½ ounces ginger beer.

Screwdriver RTR
1½ ounces vodka; 2½ ounces orange juice.

Sea-Gull
1½ ounces vodka; ½ ounce dry vermouth; ¾ ounces apricot liqueur.

Troyka
1 ounce vodka; ½ ounce Jamaica rum; 2½ ounces fresh, sweetened lemon juice—shake.

Uncle Vanya
1 ounce vodka; 2½ ounces fresh, sweetened lemon juice; ¼ ounce blackberry liqueur—shake.

Note: To make fresh, sweetened lemon juice: Mix the juice of ½ fresh lemon with 1 to 2 teaspoons of sugar to taste.

The Danish Mary and Bloody Mary recipes are for a glass, but below you will find a recipe for a quart mixture to be added to 1½ ounces of akavit or vodka in the glass as desired. We suggest that, for a party, the quart mixture be made and allowed to marinate for 24 hours before using.

Danish Mary RTR
1½ ounces akavit; the rest same as Bloody Mary mix, below.

Bloody Mary RTR
1½ ounces vodka; 3 ounces tomato juice; ¼ teaspoon Worcestershire Sauce; ¾ teaspoon fresh, sweetened lemon juice; ¾ teaspoon beef broth; pinch of salt; dash of pepper (and additional seasoning to taste).

Quart Mixture for Bloody Mary RTR and Danish Mary RTR
26 ounces tomato juice
1 ounce Worcestershire Sauce
2 ounces fresh, sweetened
  lemon juice
¾ teaspoon beef broth
pinch of salt
dash of pepper
additional seasoning to taste.
Allow to marinate for 24 hours.

Wines

We serve over 5,000 cases of "carafe" wines a year at The Russian Tea Room. "Carafe" means red and white wines that I personally select from French, Italian, Spanish, Portuguese and South American examples—the very best quality selected for balance, always leaning to the dry side. The selection of these wines changes as the market availability changes, and we usually offer two or three different white wines, and the same number of red at any one time. At the present time, for instance, we have—red: Andean Monte Tinto, Caves Dom Teodosio Pampilho, Boucheron Cuvée Rouge; white: Marino Superiore, Andean Monte Blanco, Boucheron Blanc de Blancs. They are poured into carafes for those who like to have The Russian Tea Room house wine chosen for them. Our guests trust our selections, and that is a great compliment.

Our regular wine list is a good balance of about fifty wines, which offers a wide enough selection at a considerable range of prices—four champagnes, including Chandon from California, five red Bordeaux, four white Bordeaux. We reprint The Russian Tea Room Wine List every two months, to keep it up to date, which is very important—also the shipper or importer and the vintage.

The Russian Tea Room Reserve List consists of rare and expensive wines from great vintages, such as the great growths of Bordeaux back to 1961, Corton-Charlemagne 1973, Chateau Corton Grancey 1969 and 1971, Robert Mondavi Cabernet Sauvignon Private Reserve 1971. The wines are old, the Reserve List is new—and will increase in size.

My real interest in wines began in 1967, when I took over the operation of the restaurant and started to buy wines for the first time. I took the wine course at the Sommelier Society and also had the benefit of the knowledge of several very generous wine experts in New York, who coached me through the early confusions of wine identification. Since then, with buying experience, travel to wine countries and a lot of exposure, I have come to enjoy keenly the pleasures of wine and wine knowledge. Last year I gave a series of wine tastings in the Cafe at The Russian Tea Room, which helped me very much to make wine selections for The Russian Tea Room list, especially California wines, where the innovations of new vineyards and the difficulty in finding these wines on the East Coast make the challenge even greater than buying French wines. Since these American wines are constantly improving and expanding, and international currencies are changing constantly, California will definitely be the wave of the future in American wine drinking.

Russian wines are not available aside from the sweet "Nastarovye" champagne, a machine-made product not in a class with natural champagnes. There are pleasant Moldavian, Georgian and Armenian wines—Armenia claims to be the home of the grape, where vineyards were planted by ancient Greeks thousands of years ago—but these wines must be enjoyed on their native ground. Tsinandali, a light, dry wine from Georgia, was our favorite when we visited there. In Armenia we liked the Megradzor, also white and dry—and we loved the kanyak, especially the Churchill.

Since Russian cuisine is not usually spicy, it can be complemented by many different wines. With caviar, if not vodka, then champagne or a dry, medium-bodied wine such as Pouilly Fuissé is a good choice. With Chicken Kiev, a Chardonnay or a light-bodied red Bordeaux or a young Chianti Classico would be very enjoyable. For shashlik, an older red Bordeaux or a red Burgundy, or an Italian Barolo or an older Chianti is preferable. Zakuska, or hors d'oeuvres, are very important in Russian cuisine. A flinty Chablis or Sancerre is good for the cold zakuska and could be drunk with the hot as well, but I prefer a young Bordeaux, perhaps a St. Emilion, with the hot zakuska.

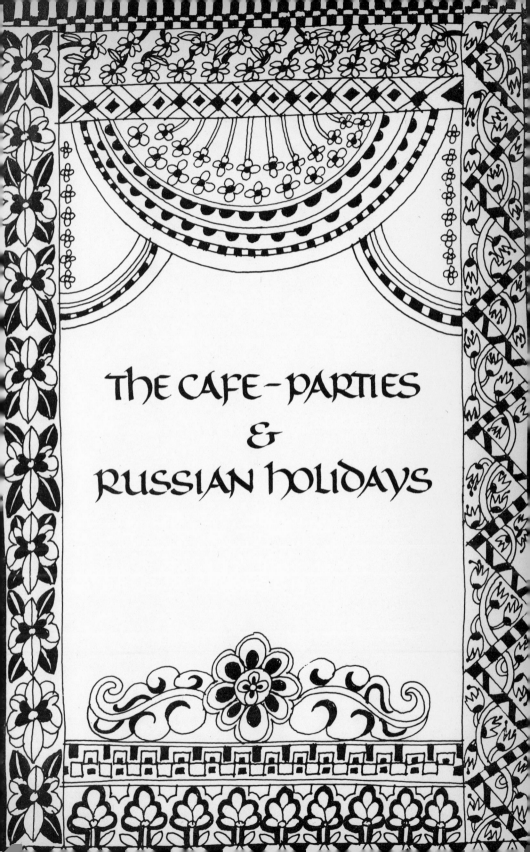

THE CAFE-PARTIES
&
RUSSIAN HOLIDAYS

At the end of 1979 we opened the Cafe at The Russian Tea Room, a glittering new room on the second floor overlooking Fifty-seventh Street. It has a beautiful etched glass window, framed by Art Deco gilded wooden curtains and set off by samovars on each side, all of which can be seen from the street below. The decor is similar to that of the main dining room, but the Café is very special—it has an opera-box look, an atmosphere of elegance enhanced by spaciousness, the paintings, the special bar—one gets the feeling of being in a fantasy world.

This feeling is reinforced by the door to the Café—a story which takes us to ancient Georgia, Leningrad, and Florence before it ends in New York.

Some years ago my husband and I visited a Georgian restaurant in Leningrad, entered by a magnificent bronze door paneled with ancient animal figures in high relief. We took a photograph of the door and then set out to duplicate it in New York. Thanks to our contractor, we found a Florentine sculptor who perfectly re-created the door. So the Café at The Russian Tea Room has one of the most beautiful and unusual entrances to be found anywhere. It just shows you can find anything in New York—including the best Russian food in the world.

And the parties in the Café are fantastic, too. There, for instance, Liza Minnelli and Mikhail Baryshnikov screened their television show "Barishnikov on Broadway" in the Café with a Zakuska party for ninety people, with four televisions sets put in for their pleasure. The Christian Brothers Winery gave a luncheon party to introduce their new Cabernet Sauvignon, and, in the music division, the Los Angeles Chamber Orchestra and the Chicago Symphony Society gave parties after their concerts at Carnegie Hall. Frank Sinatra gave a benefit party after his Carnegie Hall concert for the Police Athletic League. Mstislav Rostropovich held a cocktail party in the true Russian manner, with smoked salmon, red caviar, miniature piroshki and shashliks, herring and beets bound with sour cream on toast, and other canapés.

"American Vodka" was introduced at the Café, an occasion for which our chefs did a beautiful butter carving of Columbus's ship *Nina* on which he sailed to the New World. Carnegie Hall and Merrill Lynch gave the kick-off luncheon for the 90th Anniversary Celebration of the birth of Carnegie Hall, a gala concert and ball next door; George Balanchine had a party to announce the Tchaikovsky Festival at Lincoln Center—there have been wine tastings and vodka tastings, press parties for new movies, plays and books.

As you see, the Café is a wonderful room for private parties—a delightful and spacious place to relax and entertain friends, family, business associates, award winners, wedding guests and visiting celebrities for a leisurely luncheon, dinner or a festive supper with all the trimmings. Our chefs prepare anything from blini with caviar prepared right before your eyes and served on small plates to gloriously decorated whole salmons and hams, jewellike salads and fairy-tale cakes. Kulebiaka or Beef Stroganoff, Chicken Kiev or Karsky Shashlik— whatever you decide on will be a wonderful treat for your guests at The Russian Tea Room.

But be of good cheer if circumstances don't allow you to come to the Café in person. You may not be able to exactly re-create the loveliness and drama of the Café surroundings, but you certainly can create a festive meal like one experienced in the Café. Perhaps a brunch, a cocktail party or a dinner? All these parties are yours, as well as any other you may fancy, from the recipes in this book.

Let's take a leisurely Sunday brunch right in your own home. You might start with a fresh fruit in season, such as melon or grapefruit and follow it up with Blini with sour cream and red caviar. Or Blinchiki with Cheese, Sliced Apples or Cherry Preserves Filling, dusted with sugar and served with sour cream, would be excellent for brunch. As a change of taste, you might serve Mushrooms à la Russe, with black bread and sweet butter, to your guests. Tea with Rum, or served Russian style, with Cherry Preserves, would add a special flavor. Or as a glorious finale, you might delight your guests with Café à la Russe with Vodka or Hot Chocolate Chaliapin, with Vodka and Coffee Liqueur.

If it is to be cocktails for a few friends or for a crowd, make it a zakuska party. Look at the list of hors d'oeuvres and appetizers in this book and choose a few, many, or all of them depending on the number of guests and the variety you feel will please them. Be sure to have Blini with sour cream and red caviar, black caviar with the fixings if you can, smoked salmon, Mushrooms à la Grecque, Cucumber Salad, Kholodetz and Eggplant Orientale. Of course, each zakuska nestles in its own dish. A hot zakuska is a pleasant addition, whether it be Meatballs à la Russe or Mushrooms or Eggplant à la Russe, both gratin dishes. Hot zakuska are served from their own casserole or from a chafing dish. Don't forget the black bread and sweet butter. A selection of icy cold vodkas is essential. Chill the bottles thoroughly in the freezer, and for a delightful effect, put a bottle of vodka in a plastic bucket with water and freeze it—it will come out in an ice mold which keeps it cold and makes it exciting to serve. A surefire success at cocktail parties is a tray of sweet things, such as a selection of the pastries you find in our Dessert section.

For a proud dinner party, you might want to create a Russian Easter dinner, no matter what the season. You might start with Eggplant Orientale as an appetizer and follow it with a cup of hot or cold Borscht or Schi or any of the soups in this book. But if you have very hungry guests, treat them to a whole soup plate or bowlful, with Piroshki. The main course could be Baked Ham with Cherry Sauce or Leg of Lamb à la Russe, with glazed onions and broccoli accompanied by a Chicken Velouté Sauce. For dessert, those twin glories of Russian desserts: Kulich and Paska, followed by Café à la Russe, or espresso. You'll have a meal that is deliciously different, yet one that appeals to the most conservative of diners.

But the best of all meals is the meal that you compose yourself. We hope that the suggestions given above will inspire you to create either all-Russian feasts or occasions where you mix and match Russian and American favorites. And here is a toast for your Russian dinner:

"Za Vasha Zdarovye ee Schastyeh!"
"Health and Happiness!"

Index